Postcolonializing God

An African Practical Theology

Emmanuel Yartekwei Amugi Lartey

scm press

© Emmanuel Yartekwei Amugi Lartey 2013

Published in 2013 by SCM Press
Editorial office
3rd Floor, Invicta House
108–114 Golden Lane,
London EC1Y 0TG

SCM Press is an imprint of Hymns Ancient & Modern Ltd
(a registered charity)
13A Hellesdon Park Road
Norwich NR6 5DR, UK

www.scmpress.co.uk

All rights reserved. No part of this publication may be reproduced,
stored in a retrieval system, or transmitted,
in any form or by any means, electronic, mechanical,
photocopying or otherwise, without the prior permission of
the publisher, SCM Press.

Unless otherwise indicated, all Scripture quotations are from
The Holy Bible, English Standard version, published by
HarperCollins Publishers © 2001 by Crossway Bibles, a division of
Good News Publishers. Used by permission. All rights reserved.

The Author has asserted his right under the Copyright, Designs and
Patents Act, 1988, to be identified as the Author of this Work

British Library Cataloguing in Publication data

A catalogue record for this book is available
from the British Library

978 0 334 02982 3

Typeset by Manila Typesetting Company
Printed and bound by
Lightning Source

Contents

Introduction   vii

1   God Postcolonializes   1
2   Postcolonializing God in the USA   15
3   Postcolonializing Liturgical Practice:
    Rituals of Remembrance, Cleansing,
    Healing and Re-connection   38
4   Transcending Colonial Religion: Brother
    Ishmael Tetteh and the Etherean Mission   65
5   Postcolonializing Pastoral Care   118
6   Postcolonializing God: A Theological
    Imperative   124

Bibliography   131

Index   135

DEDICATED TO

Nunmo Amugi

(Traditional healer and spiritual consultant in the court of Gã Maŋtsɛ (King) Tackie Kome)
My paternal grandfather

Acknowledgments

I would like in the first place to give honor and praise to the Creator for grace and strength to complete this book. Additionally, there is a long line of persons to whom I am related who entered the world before me, have gone before me into the unseen realm on whose shoulders I stand, some of whom I do not even know personally. *Postcolonializing God* is dedicated to my paternal grandfather, an illustrious traditional healer and spiritual consultant, who was long gone before I entered this realm. My maternal grandfather, Christian Agbenyega Doku, who passed away when my mother was still a teenager, was a Methodist lay pastor who planted several churches along the coastal plains surrounding Accra, Ghana. I give thanks to and for each of my ancestors.

Many thanks to African mystic Brother Ishmael Tetteh, whose work the 4th chapter of this book recounts, for your spectacular contributions towards world peace in our life time. Thanks for your generous permission to cite and quote from your many books, and for your mentorship, teaching, and spiritual guidance. Your courage and creativity are an inspiration to me.

My grateful thanks go to the staff of the Association of Theological Schools (ATS) and especially the members of the Lilly Theological Research Grants Selection panel for the Lilly Theological Research Grant for 2009-10, which enabled me to secure a full year's sabbatical leave from my teaching at Candler School of Theology, Emory University to work on this book. Dr. (Ing) Emmanuel Lartey Sr., my father, passed away in September 2009 at the very beginning of my sabbatical. Honor and thanks to you, Dad, for your consistent and dedicated hard work for the newly independent nation of Ghana and on through the years. Your scholarship and commitment to our people inspire me. You taught me to think for myself and not merely to depend on convention.

Thanks are due to colleagues and students at the Candler School of Theology and the Graduate Division of Religion at Emory University who have been my dialogue partners as I have honed these thoughts and shaped my ideas into this particular work. Mention must also be made of colleagues and friends of the Society for Pastoral Theology who heard me present a draft of what is the third chapter of the book at their annual Study Conference in 2011. Thanks for your comments, critiques and feedback.

At the publishers I would like to thank Dr. Natalie Watson, Rebecca Goldsmith, Linda Crosby, Christopher Pipe as well as all others whose names I do not know, for your editorial skills and hard work. To my friends, colleagues, students, critics and conversation partners, I am very much aware that without your input, direct as well as indirect, this text would not have appeared at this time. My gratitude and thanks go to you all. My task as a practical theologian is ongoing.

Emmanuel Y. A. Lartey,
Atlanta, 2013

Introduction

Over the last century and particularly in the last 60 years, the world has seen great transformations particularly in the spheres of governance and the political control of peoples. Struggles for and processes of independence and social restructuring of once colonial countries have taken place in several parts of the globe. On the African continent following the seizure of lands and subjugation of peoples to European control in the late nineteenth century, beginning in the 1950s political governance of African countries by European powers largely came to an end, although arguably the structure of the global economic system has meant that economic control has not totally been ceded to these emergent nations. African lands that Europeans arrogated to themselves and demarcated in Berlin in 1884–5, to supply European nations with particular raw materials that would fuel their economic growth, were returned to the Africans living on those lands. African homelands had now been carved up into nation states ('countries') by Europeans. In many African countries the 1970s saw violent overthrows of the neo-colonial civilian governments that came into office at independence, replacing the European colonialists. Decades of military rule followed with attendant mismanagement and dictatorship leaving many African nations on their knees, desperately impoverished and colossally deprived. After being itself divided by differing political and economic ideologies, Germany was re-unified in 1989, when the Berlin Wall was finally torn down. The USSR collapsed as an Empire, leading to sovereignty for several nation states in the former 'Eastern Bloc'. Recently a wave of protests and agitation for change in many North African nations, dubbed the 'Arab Spring', has led to the overthrow and in some cases violent killing of officials of previously unassailable military or military-backed regimes. The Republic of South Sudan emerged in 2011 out of the larger Sudanese state following years of struggle with the northern (predominantly Arab African) people.

On the religious front the emergence of autonomous African churches from the wombs of their colonial mother-denominations was a phenomenon that began in the 1960s following decades of colonial missionary activities which flourished from the 1860s. The phenomenon of African Independent (Indigenous, Initiated or Instituted) Churches, generically referred to as AICs, swept the continent at the end of the twentieth century; practitioners and scholars saw this as evidence of the success of the missionary movement as well as the ingenuity of Africans who transposed the message of European Christianity into their own cultural forms. Debates concerning the nature of the AICs revolved around questions of authenticity, indigeneity, syncretism, inculturation, and acculturation. How does religious transmission occur? How do recipients translate, improvise, or create religious ideas and practices for themselves?

What kind of thinking and action led to the overthrow of European colonialism on the African continent? What has followed this occurrence? What has been the religious significance of autonomy for African churches? Wherein lay the appeal of the AICs? What can be said about the mega-churches which began to spring up across the continent in the 1980s? Has real religious innovation occurred? If so where and how? What does the overused word 'postcolonial' really mean, especially in practical strategic terms? In particular, what has been the religious and spiritual state of African peoples and communities through the periods of colonialism and since? How has African spirituality been involved in the experiences of colonialism and postcolonialism? Is there a postcolonial African spirituality? What shape and form does postcolonial African spirituality take? In religious terms, what are the cultural productions that have emanated from postcolonial

INTRODUCTION

African subalterns? In practical theological terms how have postcolonial Africans imaged and embodied the divine? What rituals, practices and activities have postcolonial Africans created and embodied? These are the questions that have shaped and influenced the research underlying this book and that have given it its form.

The term *postcolonial* has been utilized in many different disciplines in an attempt to capture two particular features of the global situation. First, the descriptor has been applied to the analysis of the various strategies employed by colonizers to construct images of and to exercise dominance over the colonized. This usage, mostly on the part of colonizing nations and their scholars, has been very sharply criticized.[1] Second, postcolonial criticism has referred to the study of how the colonized made use of and transcended these colonial strategies in order to articulate and assert their dignity, self-worth and identity, and to empower themselves. This way of using the term has led to a flurry of studies and texts mostly by nationals of the former colonized nations. This book can be described as presenting arguments that fall largely within this second usage.

Postcolonial has been used in a wide variety of ways. The disciplines of religion and theology have not failed to engage postcolonial studies and theories, although perhaps with not as great a volume of material as disciplines such as literature, political science or the social sciences. In the religious milieu 'postcolonial studies' have largely been used to signify a 'style of inquiry, an insight or a perspective, a catalyst, a new way of life'[2] or more poignantly as 'a collection of critical and conceptual attitudes'.[3] It is as a form of criticism that postcolonialism seems to me to be most poignant. My usage of the term as a form of criticism is

---

[1] For a detailed summary of the most trenchant critiques see Bart Moore-Gilbert, *Postcolonial Theory: Contexts, Practices, Politics*, London/New York: Verso, 1997, pp. 5–33.

[2] See R. S. Sugirtharajah, 'Charting the Aftermath: A Review of Postcolonial Criticism', in R. S. Sugirtharajah (ed.), *The Postcolonial Biblical Reader*, Oxford/Malden/Carlton: Blackwell Publishing, 2006, p. 9.

[3] Sugirtharajah, 'Charting the Aftermath', p. 9.

substantially in agreement with Edward Said, who saw criticism 'as life-enhancing and constitutively opposed to every form of tyranny, domination, and abuse, its social goals are non-coercive knowledge produced in the interests of human freedom'.[4]

I have long been perplexed by the ways in which in the fields of religion, theology and spirituality, especially in the practical disciplines within these fields, it appears to have taken a great deal of time and effort to transform the structures of thought and action implemented by the colonialists whether in the Church or in the wider community. Such transformation has been incredibly slow in coming and in many cases has hardly happened at all, the prevailing preferences of postcolonial religionists seeming to be squarely in line with colonialist teaching. Paradoxically, lately there seems rather to have been a resurgence of European supremacy in the theological and religious scholarship and practice of the African colonized and their descendants. Many African scholars and religionists seem unable to think creatively or at least independently, concerning the religions and cultures of Africa, without constantly looking over their shoulders to see what their colonial tutors and their successors might think of what they do. Much that passes as African religious studies operates with the categories and terms that were shaped and crafted by Europeans to characterize what they thought the locals were doing. Domestication appears to have taken a strong hold particularly on African theologians. In Africa to be a theologian or religious scholar meant to utilize acceptable European-derived methodologies, theories and categories in the analysis of any and every religious or cultural subject. African Christian theologians in particular have adopted colonialist discourse and method completely, and to this day evaluate their work on the basis of its fidelity to European constituted categories and methods. African theologians, religious scholars and church leaders have become the neo-colonialists of their disciplines and practices, often policing the practices of their parishioners with much stronger force

---

4 Edward W. Said, *The World, the Text, and the Critic*, London: Vintage, 1991, p. 28.

INTRODUCTION

than the European missionaries ever could or did. African church leaders have been quick to expel any whose teaching or practice departs from colonial European doctrine. The initiation of very many African Independent Churches was the result of such expulsion or debarment of Africans often because their practice was too close, in the perception of their leaders, to the precolonial African religion that had been denigrated by European colonists, or else not sufficiently in keeping with colonial dictates. European hegemony reigns supreme in African theology, very effectively enforced and carried out by African church leaders.

'Postcolonial' African Christian communities are variously described as 'immigrant churches' (in North America) and 'African-led' churches (in Europe and the UK). Here African Christian leaders have sought to provide pastoral care for persons of African descent living in the cities and centres which exported Christianity and imposed it upon their countries of origin. Actually my involvement and research revealed that by and large these communities tend to operate a colonial discourse that is strangely reminiscent of the past. They are often less progressive even than the churches in their home countries. They are in the least developed phase of any process of 'postcolonializing' God-talk and the experience of the divine. In a sense many in these churches find 'comfort' in the colonial ways of the past and never venture out of these captivities into an engagement with their context or challenge the past they have come to hold as true. They long for, promote and bask in the colonial structures that are identified with the 'heritage' of their churches.[5]

European Christianity made its mark by sharply distinguishing itself in doctrine and practice from other religious and cultural activities that Africans might engage in. African Christians have by and large imbibed this denial of their heritage and culture and continue to deny it with force. I shall be arguing that one of the hallmarks of African religious life and thought is an integrating,

---

5 In several Ghanaian Methodist congregations in the USA for example, the singing of the ancient Latin canticle 'Te Deum Laudamus', set to music by Europeans, is argued as a mark of 'authenticity' for Ghanaian Methodists, by which some leaders have sought to distinguish between true Ghanaian Methodists and unfaithful ones.

synthesizing ethos, whereas European Christianity has progressed by separation and analysis, distinguishing itself from beliefs and practices that differ from its own, labelling them as 'evil', 'demonic', 'dangerous' or else unsavoury, barbaric or unenlightened. By means of hierarchy and fear-mongering, European Christianity has succeeded in misinterpreting, misappropriating and mischaracterizing much of African life and thought. Educated Africans have been bullied into accepting such characterizations of their own life and heritage on pain of being seen as at best uneducated and at worst promoting dangerous superstitions that will lead to an eternity in the fires of hell by all who do not escape them. Such characterization has left many African scholars cowering and has prevented much creative engagement with the rich cultural and religious heritage of the African world. Cameroonian philosopher and historian Achille Mbembe's comment regarding subjection by postcolonial rulers in the 'postcolony' aptly characterizes this phenomenon. He writes:

> If subjection appears more intense than it might be, this is because the subjects of the *commandement* have internalized authoritarian epistemology to the point where they have reproduced it themselves in all the minor circumstances of daily life – social networks, cults and secret societies, culinary practices, leisure activities, modes of consumption, styles of dress, rhetorical devices, and the whole political economy of the body.[6]

'Internalized authoritarian epistemology' of European origin truly characterizes the work of African theologians and scholars of African religion and the liturgical and practical activities of many African churches. *Postcolonializing God* is born out of a strong desire to depart from the sterile paralysis in postcolonial African religious and theological practice by highlighting and discussing areas where courageous and innovative postcolonial religious and practical theological work is being done.

---

6 Achille Mbembe, *On the Postcolony*, Berkeley/Los Angeles/London: University of California Press, 1991, p. 128.

INTRODUCTION

To do so, and thus emphasize a dynamic process, I have chosen to reformulate the term 'postcolonial' and to cast it into active voice in two ways, namely as an adjective and a verb. As an adjective, 'postcolonializing' qualifies the divine, offering thoughts describing an aspect of the nature of God. In this sense, the study is of ways in which God may be seen to be present and active in the world. God is viewed in this usage as active, involved and in interaction with humans. God is seen as one who, in keeping with the divine nature, acts to decolonize, diversify and promote counter-hegemonic social conditions. As a verb 'postcolonializing' articulates the nature, acts and activities of communities, leaders or people who seek to establish communities of faith or else who produce or provide regularly or occasionally rituals or ceremonies that, reflecting the decolonizing nature of the divine, are plural in form, diverse in character and which subvert and overturn the hegemonic conditions established through colonialism creating forms of spiritual engagement that more truly reflect categories of thought and life that emanate from an African, rather than a European, way of being and thinking.

The Bible depicts the divine as active in the creation, recreation and sustaining of the world, and this has had significant influence upon African peoples since the end of the twentieth century. The first chapter of this book explores passages in both the Hebrew Scriptures and the Christian Testament that depict divine action as promoting of diversity. The second chapter discusses the African American (Black) Church as an example of the postcolonializing activities of Africans enslaved in the Americas.

The third chapter presents an analysis of a ceremony of healing and reconciliation which was held in Elmina, Ghana, in 2007 in the bicentennial year following the abolition of the Transatlantic slave trade. This communal liturgy attracted diasporan Africans from across the globe and was constructed with the aim of ritually cleansing and restoring relations amongst Africans whose ancestors had been complicit as well as victims of the heinous trade.

My search for creative postcolonializing African Christian communities yielded very little. The vast majority of the diasporan African Churches I engaged can only be described as postcolonial in the historical sense of existing *after* colonialism. They can by no means be described as engaging in postcolonializing practices. Nevertheless, a mystical community which was started some 35 years ago in Ghana is one of the most exciting examples of the postcolonializing activities of people of African faith. This community, the Etherean Mission, is given its first full exposition within an academic context here in the fourth chapter of this book.

Chapter 5 explores postcolonial African practices in pastoral care and the book ends with a consideration of differences between imitation, improvisation and creativity, and the future of postcolonializing activities engaged in by Africans worldwide.

Postcolonial criticism has been fuelled by scholars of Asian and Middle Eastern origins (i.e. specifically, Homi Bhabha, Gayatri Spivak, and Edward Said). Many of the seminal works, though, reflect the African and African diasporan postcolonial experience (e.g. Aimé Césaire, Frantz Fanon, Albert Memmi, Chinua Achebe, Ngugi wa Thiong'o). This book concentrates upon African and African diasporan scholarship and experience in order to emphasize, contribute to, articulate and focus attention on the African postcolonial experience, which, though sharing many common features with other former colonized people, has particularities that must not be lost sight of.

Characteristics of postcolonializing activities

I was born in the twilight years of British colonial rule in the West African colony which Europeans named 'the Gold Coast'. I come to discuss and theorize colonization and its lingering effects as well as postcolonial oppositional practices, informed by my own experience. My early experience of education was in an English-speaking church-established primary (elementary) school. This was followed by a Methodist mission-founded boys' boarding school for secondary (high) school education. After graduation from the University in Ghana I proceeded to the UK for graduate studies. I have since been an educator in Ghana, Britain, in other European countries, and in the USA. Meanwhile I have travelled extensively and engaged in research and study in many different parts of the world. Throughout my life I have had the honour and privilege of interacting closely with colonizers and colonized, neo-colonizers and neo-colonized, and with persons whose desire and activities can be described as postcolonializing.[7] Aimé Césaire's classic brief essay *Discourse on Colonialism* reveals a reversal of effect that has been instructive for me in my investigations into this subject. Césaire is worth quoting extensively:

> Colonization . . . dehumanizes even the most civilized man; that colonial activity, colonial enterprise, colonial conquest, which is based on contempt for the native and justified by that contempt, inevitably tends to change him who undertakes it; that the colonizer, who in order to ease his conscience gets into the habit of seeing the other man as *an animal*, accustoms himself to treating him like an animal, and tends objectively to transform *himself* into an animal. It is this result, this boomerang effect of colonization that I wanted to point out.[8]

My study has included Césaire's 'boomerang effect' on colonizer as well as neo-colonial and postcolonial autocrats. In this book my emphasis is on transforming the deleterious effects of colonization through postcolonializing activities of postcolonial agents. My personal experience has been informed and dialogically engaged with extensive reading of colonial, neo-colonial and postcolonial literature, theoretical as well as fictional, and in different disciplines. Out of these rich, challenging, alienating and illuminating engagements emerge my views on the characteristics of postcolonializing discourse and practice.

What then are some of the characteristics of African postcolonializing activities specifically in regard to practical theology and

---

7 Albert Memmi's seminal book, *The Colonizer and the Colonized*, written out of the North African colonial experience, carefully explores the effects of colonization upon both colonizer and colonized.
8 Aimé Césaire, *Discourse on Colonialism*, translated by Joan Pinkham, New York: Monthly Review Press, 1972, p. 41. Both Memmi and Césaire are exceedingly illuminating on the effects of colonization on colonizers.

religious practice? I will be arguing that the following are some of the marks by which one may begin to identify positive postcolonializing activities taking place in African continental and diasporan communities. I argue that it is possible to see divine action in the world in terms of postcolonializing activities. My theological inclination is to see God as it were as having been at work postcolonializing relations and situations of peoples in the world. Human persons have also been engaged synergistically in these postcolonializing activities in concert with the Divine. Process theological thought is attractive to me in this recognition of divine and human synergy. However, it is perhaps, as will be clear as the work enfolds, African religious thinking that is the most energizing influence on my own thinking. I recognize and discuss the seven features that follow:

First, postcolonializing activities are *counter-hegemonic*, insurgent, even subversive in nature and character. By their very nature they call into question dominance and hegemony in human relations. Where patterns of dominance have solidified into hegemonic structures, these activities take the form of insurgency and may be deemed subversive by the powers that be. They aim to disrupt and subvert dominant structures in order to promote more equitable relations between people. Many who suffered colonialism's brutal suppression resorted to forms of domesticated discourse as a survival strategy. These forms of discourse appear innocuous but are laced with counter-hegemonic themes that call into question the strategies and processes colonialists use to promote their values and denigrate those of the colonized. As such, domesticated discourse is a latent postcolonializing activity. More overt forms of counter-hegemonic activity are also discernible. Both latent and overt counter-hegemonic practices deserve attention as postcolonializing activities.

Second, postcolonializing activities are *strategic*. In other words they bring into critical focus the dialogical nature of relations between theory and practice, and result in actions with transformative intent in the world. In this sense they may be termed praxiological or practical-and-theoretical with an action-for-change orientation. These activities at times are overtly political, at other

INTRODUCTION

times quietist. However, in all cases the agents of postcolonializing activities are reflective practitioners of their disciplines and arts. They are also motivated by the desire for transformation. Postcolonializing activities are not engaged in from the safe, disinterested and uninvolved distance of purported objective research. The postcolonializer is by no means a disinterested observer. Instead, in an incarnational sense, they are *intentional* and *involved*. Postcolonializing activities betray an interested commitment to involvement with the issues and subjects affected by oppressive colonizing actions, and are engaged in with the express intention of seeking transformed existence for all.

Third, postcolonializing activities are themselves *hybrid* and they promote multi-dimensional discourses and practices. They are deeply *variegated* and *plural*. *Diversity* is a hallmark and desired end of postcolonializing processes. As such they are *messy*, in that they question and disrupt sharp and clear boundaries between materials, recognizing the often arbitrary lines of demarcation that are drawn, and calling for attention to complexity and *metissage* in the approach to all matters. Sharp demarcations and neat contents are not to be found in postcolonializing discourse and practices. They are therefore also and always ambiguous and at times contradictory, full of controversy, wary of over-privileging any one form over all others.

Fourth, postcolonializing activities, in engagement with the previous features, are deeply *interactional* and *intersubjective*. They emphasize the social and global nature of phenomena and encourage approaches to subjects that engage interactively with all people's experience in the discourse on any subject. In other words they engage analytically and relationally with the agents as well as the practices they wish to critique and transform. Relationality is valued especially when it is set within an ethical framework of equality and respect.

Fifth, postcolonializing activities are *dynamic* in nature. They recognize that issues are in a constant state of change and flux. As such they attempt to engage in analyses that reflect time, change and movement. Analysing moving structures can be daunting. However, recognizing that social reality is inevitably fluid is a sign of maturity not to be rejected. Postcolonializing practices presuppose and therefore prepare for change.

Sixth, postcolonializing activities are *polyvocal*. Both the Babel and the Pentecost narratives in the Bible recognize and encourage many voices to speak and be heard on the subjects under consideration. Never satisfied with just one perspective on any subject, the postcolonializer actively seeks out other voices, especially submerged, ignored or rejected voices, to be invited to articulate their own authentic voice. Subjugated voices with despised knowledge are given room at the postcolonial table. Educated, middle-class, liberal, progressive voices are not the only ones invited to speak. Nor is there an attempt to silence the speech of the uneducated, differently able or different.

Seventh and finally, postcolonializing activities are *creative*. They call for and produce new forms of being, institutions and practices. They entail a weaving together of disparate materials into innovative forms and practices. *Creativity moves* beyond improvisation (which implies utilizing the left-overs from the colonial project in the formulation of structures that implicitly are temporary). It requires the generation and utilization of new practices, methods and material in the development and promotion of substantially different forms of activity that go beyond the status quo inherited or established as standard by colonizers.

Historical routes

African historian Adu Boahen, in a highly informative classic study, has analysed the reactions and responses of Africans to the European colonialist project. Adu Boahen divides the colonial era into three distinct periods. First, the 1890s to the end of the First World War; then 1919–35; and finally 1935 to the 1960s. Adu Boahen focuses on the first two for in-depth scrutiny. He shows how during those years, far from being the activity solely of the educated elite, anti-colonialist reactions and organizing 'extended to all classes, and groups of Africans, the traditional as well as the educated elite, illiterate farmers and traders, merchant

INTRODUCTION

princes and civil servants, rural as well as urban dwellers'.[9] In the rural areas, the chosen means of African resistance were rebellions and insurrections against the colonial systems of taxation, compulsory cultivation of crops, land alienation, tyrannical behaviour of colonial officials and denigration of African culture and traditional ways of life.

Adu Boahen does not fail to observe what many scholars have often overlooked, namely the role of religion in the anti-colonial endeavours. Given the pervasive nature of African religion in the lives of the populace, this should really come as no surprise. Priests, priestesses and 'spirit mediums' of the religious traditions of Africa were deeply involved in and on occasion led these insurrections against the Europeans. In the Congo, the priestess Maria Nkoie gave her followers charms to make them immune to European guns and led them in a revolt which lasted from 1916 till 1921. In East Africa the most well-known rebellion was the Maji Maji rebellion which broke out in 1905 under the leadership of the traditional prophet Kinjikitile Ngwale. There was also the rebellion of 1913 inspired by the Mumbo cult leader Onyango Dande.

Adu Boahen demonstrates how rebellions, migrations and passive resistance (including refusals to comply with orders, absenteeism, feigned illness, work slowdowns and rejection of the European instituted systems of education) were adopted by the rural populace in their resistance of European domination. All of these activities were brutally suppressed and several thousand Africans lost their lives. The educated elite and urban workers typically adopted a strategy of reform rather than attempted overthrow of the European colonial system. One major instrument of protest and criticism of the educated elite was the press. Adu Boahen observes that between 1890 and 1919 about ten newspapers were founded in Ghana and five in Nigeria. In South Africa, as early as 1884, J. T. Jabavu founded the first African newspaper, *Imvozaba Ntsundu* (Native Opinion) and by 1915 there were five

---

9 A. Adu Boahen, *African Perspectives on Colonialism*, Baltimore, MD: The Johns Hopkins University Press, 1987, p. 63.

major African newspapers there. In addition a 'number of societies, associations, and political parties were formed during this period to lead the campaign against the colonial system'.[10] Notable amongst these are the Aborigines' Rights Protection Society (ARPS) founded in Cape Coast, Ghana in 1897; the Young Senegalese Club in 1910; and the Peoples Union (1910) and the Anti-Slavery and Aborigines Society (1912) formed in Nigeria by educated elite and traditional rulers.

Besides associations and parties, the other channels used by the African educated elite in their anticolonial campaigns were independent Christian churches. Boahen categorizes these into two types, namely the Ethiopian and the millenarian or Pentecostal. The former emphasized African self-improvement, self-rule and political rights and the latter an apocalyptic vision of divine intervention, possession by the Holy Spirit, healings, prophecies and other gifts of the Spirit. The Ethiopian church movements were particularly strong in southern and central Africa while the Pentecostal churches (referred to in the region as 'spiritual' churches) flourished in western Africa. Examples of the Ethiopian include Nehemiah Tile's 'Tembu church' (founded in South Africa in 1884) and the South African Ethiopian church founded by Willie J. Mokalapa in 1892. Tile, originally converted to Wesleyan Methodism, formed his own church movement as a result of his strong nationalist and anti-colonialist sentiments.

Knowledge of the histories of these churches founded by Africans in the last decades of the nineteenth century demonstrates that they were as anti-colonial as they were anti-missionary, a fact which led historians Oliver and Atmore to the opinion that Christian-educated Africans were the first African nationalists.[11] Such a view, however, ignores the many uneducated ordinary Africans who resisted, rebelled or else surreptitiously continued their own practices and beliefs throughout the European occupation of African lands.

---

10 Boahen, *African Perspectives on Colonialism*, p. 68.
11 Boahen, *African Perspectives on Colonialism*, p. 74. See R. Oliver & A. Atmore, *Africa since 1800*, Cambridge: Cambridge University Press, 1967, p. 157.

INTRODUCTION

During the second period (1919–35), more Ethiopian and Zionist churches emerged across the continent than in the first period, especially in southern and central Africa. In South Africa, for example, the number of such churches rose from 76 in 1918 to 320 by 1932 and in Mozambique from 76 in 1918 to over 380 in 1938. Significant in the appeal of these churches was their emphasis on African self-improvement and political rights. They provided avenues for ordinary people to express their hostility to the new colonial social structures. Many preached and promoted pride in African culture and challenged the European mission-related churches for their hypocrisy and condemnation of African culture, collusion with colonial oppressors and racial discrimination.

The Kimbanguist and Kitawala churches started in Lower Congo and Eastern Congo in the then 'Belgian Congo' in 1921 and 1923–5 were among the most radical and powerful anti-colonial church movements. Simon Kimbangu, a Bakongo catechist, founded the Kimbanguist church, declaring himself a prophet sent by God to deliver Africans from colonial rule. Kimbangu was arrested on 14 September 1921 and exiled to Katanga, where he died 30 years later. In spite of this, the Kimbanguist church spread very rapidly and continues today, now perhaps ironically a member of the World Council of Churches, to be a significant voice for AICs across the continent and globe. The Kitawala church was founded by Tomo Nyirenda in 1923 in Katanga province and spread rapidly through the region. Nyirenda fled from the Belgian Congolese authorities into then Northern Rhodesia in 1926, but was arrested by the British there and eventually executed. However, as with the Kimbanguists, the killing of the prophet only served to accelerate the growth and spread of the movement.

There is evidence that practitioners of African indigenous religions also challenged the colonial system. The 'Mumbo cult' (founded in 1913) and that established by Ndonye wa Kauti (in 1922) are examples of these.[12] In West Africa the Musama Disco Christo Church (founded in Ghana in 1922) is an example of a creative AIC which developed a brand of Christianity in

---

12 Boahen, *African Perspectives on Colonialism*, p. 89.

active interaction with Akan social, cultural, religious and political structures while championing and modelling the cause of African self-government.[13]

There is clearly a trajectory of African religious and spiritual resistance to colonial subjection which emerged in very swift response to the establishment of colonial rule across the continent. This brief excursus into African history has sought to establish this fact. Postcolonializing activity sponsored, promulgated and engaged in by religious personages is evidently a long and established African tradition. However, in the second chapter I discuss this historical development, noting that the power of these movements was eclipsed after independence as their quest for political and global legitimacy increased. The hegemonic discourses of European Christianity seem to have succeeded in placing icy hands on the innovativeness of African religious leaders. Where the elimination of prophetic leaders proved ineffective in damping down movements for self-realization, domestication through hegemonic socio-cultural, educational and political means appears to have succeeded.

In the first chapter I wish to explore the postcolonializing impulses that appear to be present in the scriptures of the Hebrews and of Christianity. In these scriptures strands of thought, narratives and practices appear in which God postcolonializes social, political and religious circumstances. This turn to the scriptures not only recognizes a postcolonializing God but also is itself a postcolonializing activity. Postcolonializers typically employ the tools and resources utilized by the colonizers but do so in subversive, critical and counter-hegemonic ways. The impulse is also a theological one. These texts suggest divine activities that can themselves be described as postcolonializing. It is this depiction of God as postcolonializer that I find compelling and very germane to this discussion.

---

13 For a detailed study of the Musama Disco Christo Church (MDCC) see my research published in Emmanuel Y. Lartey, *Pastoral Counselling in Inter-cultural Perspective*, Frankfurt/London/New York: Peter Lang, 1987, pp. 181–226.

I

God Postcolonializes

And what is Christianity but a great hybrid, comprised at the urban crossroads of the Roman Empire? It exploded into mission on Pentecost: A vision of a multilingual understanding dancing in dissident flames upon the heads of its first community.[1]

A postcolonial reading of the 'Tower of Babel' story

The aetiological story recorded in Genesis 11.1–9 seeks to offer a narrative explanation of the diversity, especially in languages, observable in the world. The story is of a migratory people united in language travelling from the east and settling – doubtlessly for a period until the resources for sustenance ran out – in a fertile plain. These migratory people appear to have found a place where they might settle for a significant duration of time. Alongside their desire to 'settle' (v. 4c 'lest we be dispersed over the face of the whole earth') is also a wish to be remembered and honoured by their descendants (v. 4b 'let us make a name – *shem* – for ourselves'). For this reason they may be described as 'Shemites', a people seeking to make a name for themselves. 'Colonialism', declares Brazilian-born US theologian Vítor Westhelle, 'operates by interest (i.e. financial gain) but is motivated by desire to make a name for oneself'.[2] Their chosen means of achieving these goals was to 'build

---

[1] Catherine Keller, Michael Nausner & Mayra Rivera (eds), *Postcolonial Theologies: Divinity and Empire*, St Louis, MO: Chalice Press, 2004, p. 13.

[2] Vitor Westhelle, *After Heresy: Colonial Practices and Postcolonial Theologies*, Eugene, OR: Cascade Books, p. 8.

a city and a tower' (v. 4a). Their settling in one place bespeaks their desire to uphold a unity of place. So as to ensure that they are not scattered they appeal to the security of being in one place. They embark on a project to make themselves great, be remembered as a powerful people, remain securely in one place and be a united people. Now, none of these desires can be construed as being ignoble in itself. Troublesome, exacting and rather a humbug ('hubris') perhaps, but by no means dishonourable or destructive. These 'Shemites' (name seekers), then, are seeking security of place, greatness of name and the power of oneness, without reference to or relationship with the God of All Creation, whose wishes and purposes in creation they appear to have lost sight of.

The narrative continues by asserting that YHWH comes down to visit and take a look at what they had built, perhaps, as the story implies, disturbed by the tower which had its top 'in the heavens' (v. 4a) suggesting an intrusion into the heavenly realm. YHWH's curiosity has been ignited by that which the 'children of man' (v. 5) had built. The divine response is both enigmatic and purposeful. It is premised on the unity of the people and especially their one language. This kind of unity and oneness of language has given them the means to intrude upon the divine realm. The Shemites are seeking for themselves that which transcends the bounds of their humanity in relationship to God, while also flying in the face of the divine will and desire for all humanity. Here, on a postcolonial reading of this story, it is my view that what the Creator recognizes in the resolve of the Shemites is a departure from the diversity of creation. The oneness of language and culture had produced a hegemonic, power-hoarding, name-seeking group of humans whose intention to dominate would be unchallenged (v. 6). Their desire to control, dominate and conquer all, even the heavenly realm, would be unstoppable. The divine purpose implicit in the diversity of all creation, that there would be 'checks and balances', many different voices to listen to, and a range of possible cultures to embrace, had been endangered. The variety that was intended to be the characteristic of humanity was at risk. Instead of 'filling the whole earth' (Gen. 1.28), the express desire and purpose of the Creator repeated to Noah and his family after the Flood (Gen. 9.1), these people wanted to settle and not be dispersed throughout the earth. This group of humans desired total control, hegemony, prime place currently and for posterity. They would debase and obliterate any differences among them – in point of fact they would not allow or recognize any differences. They had one language. They would insist on their way alone as being the way for all to follow. This is the essence of colonization. The language, customs and ways of life of one group are imposed on all. Everyone who comes under the influence of the colonizer must succumb to the colonizer's way or else be crushed. Everyone must 'speak the same language' – a supremely monoculturalist insistence – or be brought into line, forcibly if necessary, eliminated, expelled or else considered uncultured, uncouth, deviant even deranged. God, the Creator of diversity, cannot abide such hegemonic control. God 'confuses (*babel*) their language' (v. 7). Now each must have their own voice. Each must speak for themselves. The many voices of creation would sound again. God also disperses them over all the earth. God pluralizes their discourse, their culture and their manner of life. The diversity of creation is re-affirmed. The 'filling of the whole earth' is promoted. This action of God has been interpreted by many commentators as 'punishment'. It need not be punitive. Moreover, it need not be seen as the action of a fearful, insecure deity. Instead I see this divine action as a re-affirmation of the purpose of creation, a revalorizing of the diversity built into the very sinews of creation.

In postcolonial terms, at least three lessons can be derived from this narrative. First, that the existing diversity of human languages and cultures is the result of divine redemptive action. God acts to ensure that there is diversity in humanity's culture. Second, that diversity is preferred by God to hegemony. Unity or uniformity directed towards the *hubris* of intrusive power and self- (or people-) aggrandizing control contradicts the Creator's will and purpose in humanity. Stated simply – God prefers diversity. Third, that God acts within the global community to affirm human diversity. God is not inactive in the face of hegemonic control by any human community. God acts to dispel and diffuse hegemony. God not only decolonizes (scatters the people) but also *post*colonizes (confuses the language) of human community. It is as such perhaps in the confusing (*babel*) of the language of the people that we see most clearly the postcolonializing intent of God. Language, one of the most salient characteristics of culture and politics, is what is diversified, symbolic of God's counter-hegemonic and pluralizing activity.

Jesus and people of other faiths: Practical theology and religious pluralism in the Gospels

One intriguing aspect of the life of Jesus portrayed for us in the Gospels has to do with his encounters with people of different faiths. On several occasions, and we shall consider only four here, Jesus either meets with a person of a faith other than his own Jewish tradition or else he makes reference to people of other faiths in stories and parables he tells to illustrate his teaching.

I am approaching these testimonies of Jesus' encounters with people of differing faiths as a practical theologian and so do so with the methodologies most favoured by practical theologians. Practical theologians typically recognize that the starting point of their practice as well as their academic work lies in the exigencies of people's experiences of life – especially life's pains, sorrows, losses, traumas and disasters. Pastoral theologians in particular seem to deal mostly with experiences of pain and loss. Occasionally the joys as well, but by and large pastoral theologians come into the picture most critically when and where there is or has been some suffering, loss or tragedy. The experience, the case study, the self report, the client's narrative – these are the points of entry for most pastoral care (and counselling) as well as pastoral theological work. My pastoral theological work tends to flow in a pastoral cycle that I have described in the following way.[3]

---

3 See *In Living Colour: An Intercultural Approach to Pastoral Care and Counselling*, London: Jessica Kingsley, 2003, pp. 131–3.

Situational analysis ↔ Theological analysis → Critique of theology

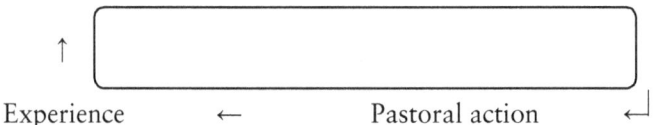

Experience ← Pastoral action

Although any of the nodal points in this diagram could notionally be the starting point, more often than not the experiential tends to be the point of entry into the pastoral cycle. I am always at pains to point out that regardless of the starting point it is imperative, if a truly pastoral engagement is desired, that all the phases (or stations) in the cycle be 'performed' or gone through. As I have pondered the issue of religious pluralism, an increasingly observable feature of our postcolonial global scene, I have found it useful to start with a theological mediation, specifically an exploration of the Gospels, Christian scriptural references that report directly on the practice, experience and life style of Jesus of Nazareth. For Christians these texts are foundational for their life, faith and practice. It is illuminating therefore to ask, 'What was Jesus' attitude to persons of other religious faiths? How do the Gospels portray Jesus in the practice of engaging people of faiths other than his own?' For many Christians this is a question they warm to. It finds resonance with their theological orientation to life. I find however that they have hardly ever been asked or else asked themselves these particular questions in relation to the following Gospel texts, and they are often at a loss as to how to begin to address them.

Let us look at *four* New Testament pericopes that introduce Jesus' interactions with or reference to persons of different religious and ethnic origins, namely: the Roman centurion (Matt. 8.5–13; Luke 7.1–10); the Canaanite (Syro-Phoenician) woman (Matt. 15.21–8; Mark 7.24–30); the Samaritan leper (Luke 17.11–19) and Jesus' parable of the 'Good' Samaritan (Luke 10.30–7). The point of referring to these Gospel stories is that in each of them Jesus encounters or engages someone of a different religious tradition than his own.

The greatest faith in Israel: A Roman centurion (Matt. 8.5–13)

It is very likely that the Roman centurion encountered in this story adhered to a form of the Roman religion practised at the time. Roman religion in the time of Jesus was conceived of and practised as a contractual relationship between humans and the forces believed to control people's existence and well-being. Roman religion was a mixture of rituals, taboos, traditions and observances gathered over the years from a number of different sources. The result of such religious attitudes was two particular forms of practice. One, *a state cult* which had influence on political and military events, and the other a *private/domestic practice* in which the head of the family oversaw rituals and prayers in a manner analogous to the way representatives of the people performed public ceremonials. A *pontifex maximus* headed up Roman state religion with a pontifical college made up of the *rex sacrorum* (chief of rites and rituals), *pontifices* (priests), *flamines* (priests to individual gods) – with the *flamen dialis* (the priest of Jupiter) at the head, and the *vestal virgins*, who kept the flame of religion alive through their virginity and ongoing chastity.

Most of the Roman gods and goddesses were a blend of several religious influences. The Greek and the Roman pantheon looked very similar but for different names. Ancient Egyptian gods and goddesses were often also identified with them. Religious festivals were held throughout the year, the earliest forms being games. The commonest form of religious activity for the Romans required some kind of sacrifice, usually animal sacrifice. Worship of dead ancestors by families during the *parentilia* in the month of February was a deeply sacred occurrence. Since Roman religion was not founded on some core belief which ruled out other religions, foreign religions, e.g. the goddess Cybele (circa 204 BC) and the worship of the Egyptian gods Isis (Auset) and Osiris (Asar) (beginning of the first century BC), found it relatively easy to establish themselves in the imperial capital itself.

While the text does not specifically name the type of practice the Roman centurion was engaged in, in all likelihood he was a participant to some degree in the religion of his nation, culture and time period. In spite of the mélange that probably constituted his religious practice and its marked difference from the Jewish faith of Jesus, the Roman centurion is held up as an *ideal exemplar of faith*. Surprisingly, without urging him to repudiate his faith or convert to the faith Jesus proclaimed and lived, Jesus says: 'Truly, I tell you, in no one in Israel have I found such faith' (Matt. 8.10). This must have been a tantalizing statement to many. On a postcolonial reading, however, it suggests that Jesus was far more ready to recognize faithfulness wherever (and in whomever) he found it and to be less concerned about having everyone believe in the same way. The faith being commended was indeed faith in Jesus. However it was coming from a very different culture, nationality and religious heritage. It was from a foreigner, an uncircumcised, oppressive foreigner at that. Yet, Jesus finds no greater faith among his own.

Challenging and correcting the Master: The Syro-Phoenician woman (Matt. 15.21–8)

The Syro-Phoenician woman who came to Jesus most likely adhered to the Canaanite religion of her place of origin and time. The Canaanites were a sophisticated agricultural and urban people. They were a people who absorbed and assimilated the features of many cultures of the ancient Near East for at least 500 years before the Israelites entered their area of control. Canaanite religion was an agricultural religion with pronounced fertility motifs. Their main gods were called the *Baalim* (i.e. Lords) and their consorts the *Baalot* (Ladies) or *Asherah* (singular), usually known by the personal plural name *Ashtoret*. The *Baalim* and the *Baalot*, gods and goddesses of the earth, were believed to be the revitalizers of the forces of nature upon which agriculture depended. The revitalization process involved a sacred marriage, replete with sexual, both symbolic and actual, activities between men, representing the *Baalim*, and sacred temple prostitutes (*qedeshot*), representing the *Baalot*. Cultic ceremonies involving sexual acts between male members of the agricultural communities and sacred prostitutes dedicated to the *Baalim* were focused on the Canaanite concept of sympathetic magic. As the *Baalim* (through the actions of selected men) both symbolically and actually impregnated the sacred prostitutes in order to reproduce in kind, so also, it was believed, the *Baalim* (as gods of the weather and the earth) would send the rains (often identified with semen) to the earth so that it might yield abundant harvests of grains and fruits. As the Canaanites and the Israelites began to live in closer contact with each other the faith of Israel tended to absorb some of the concepts and practices of Canaanite religion. Some Israelites, for instance, began to name their children after the Baalim; even one of Israel's great and revered judges, Gideon, was also known by the name Jerubbaal ('Let Baal contend' Judges 6.32).

The woman who came to Jesus was Syro-Phoenician by ethnicity/nationality and Canaanite by religion. Yet, she engaged Jesus in revelatory and challenging ways that some argue transformed Jesus' attitude towards those he and other Jews referred to derogatorily as 'dogs'. She clearly outwitted Jesus, making use of his own tradition to press her case for healing attention for her daughter. At the end of their encounter Jesus declares of her, 'Woman, great is your faith' (Matt. 15.28a). Here also there is no requirement for conversion or repudiation of her Canaanite religion. Jesus recognizes and adulates her persistent faith that would not take no for an answer, a faith derived from a different religious context. She clearly approaches Jesus out of the realms of her own tradition and implicitly rebukes Jesus for his narrow focus and interpretation of his mission.

In postcolonializing terms, she expands the mission and universalizes the brief of the message of Jesus. Jesus has to reappraise his focus and recognize that there are others, not of his ethnic and religious tradition, outside of the empire, who also are the children of God. The woman's rebuke, 'even the dogs eat the crumbs that fall from their masters' table' (Matt. 15.27), represents postcolonializing at a very significant level. Accepting for argument's sake the racially, ethnically and politically demeaning presumptions of the assumptive world adopted by Jesus, she subverts the rhetoric and employs it to challenge the Master's own ministry and life purpose, causing him to acknowledge that by the logic of his own prejudiced stance he had to act differently. This was the way in which those who fought for the independence of African nations from colonial rule utilized the colonialists' own presuppositions to undo the burdens of domination. This was what Martin Luther King Jr did when in the 'I have a Dream' speech he spoke about America's uncashed cheque.

The grateful foreigner (Luke 17.11–19) and the 'Good' Samaritan (Luke 10.29–37)

Samaritan religion was parallel to but very separate from Judaism. Samaritans claim their worship, based on the Samaritan Torah, is the true religion of the ancient Israelites prior to the Babylonian Exile, preserved by those who remained in the land of Israel – as opposed to Judaism, which they assert is a related but altered and amended religion brought back by the exiled returnees. Ancestrally claiming descent from a group of Israelite inhabitants who have connections to ancient Samaria from the beginning of the Babylonian Exile, they derive their name from the Hebrew term 'Keepers of the Law'.

According to Samaritan tradition, Mount Gerizim was the original Holy Place of the Israelites from the time that Joshua conquered Canaan and the twelve tribes settled the land. The Samaritans insist that they are the direct descendants of the Northern Israelite tribes of Ephraim and Manasseh, who survived the destruction of the Northern Kingdom of Israel by the Assyrians in 722 BC. Jewish tradition maintains a different origin for the Samaritans. The Talmud mentions a people called 'Cuthim' on a number of occasions, mentioning their arrival by the hands of the Assyrians. According to 2 Kings 17 and Josephus (*Antiquities* 9.277–91) the people of Israel were removed by the king of the Assyrians who then brought people from Babylon, Cuthah, Avah, Emath and Sepharvaim to places in Samaria. When the Judean exile ended in 538 BC, according to the Jewish version of events, and the exiles began returning home from Babylon, they found their former homeland populated by other people who claimed the land as their own and Jerusalem, their former glorious capital, in ruins.

The precise date of the schism between Samaritans and Jews is unknown, but was certainly complete by the end of the fourth century BC. Archaeological excavations at Mount Gerizim suggest that a Samaritan temple was built there around 330 BC. According to Samaritans, it was on Mount Gerizim that Abraham offered Isaac in human sacrifice (Gen. 22). The Torah mentions the place where God *will choose* to establish his name (Deut. 12.5) and Judaism takes this to refer to Jerusalem. However, the Samaritan text speaks of the place where God *has chosen* to establish his name and Samaritans identify it as Mount Gerizim, making it the focus of their spiritual life.

Samaritan religion is based on some of the same books as mainstream Judaism, but differs from the latter. Basic beliefs of the Samaritans include the unity of Hashem and careful avoidance of anthropomorphic references to Hashem. They affirm that Moses is the only true prophet and there will be none like him. They therefore reject any scripture other than the Torah. Samaritans maintain that Mount Gerizim is the Holy Mount and believe in a coming Taheb (restorer or Messiah) who will restore the period of favour with Hashem.

Samaritan religion, then, though based on similar texts and traditions, was quite different from and in several respects antagonistic to the Jewish faith of Jesus. Nevertheless, Jesus identifies the returning grateful healed leper as 'a foreigner' (Luke 17.18) – without specifying his *religious* otherness. Interestingly, however, when called upon to answer the question, 'who is my neighbour?' Jesus chooses a Samaritan above a priest and a Levite, with a veiled implication about religion (priest, Levite, Samaritan) as the example of true neighbourliness worthy of emulation in his narrative response (Luke 10.29–37). No doubt to the chagrin and annoyance of his Jewish hearers, Jesus lifts up the despised Samaritan as the example of true faith and ethical practice.

In this story, then, Jesus is the one who himself engages in postcolonializing discourse. He points to the most unexpected (by his hearers) and unlikely people (in the estimation of his own dominant compatriots) as the exemplars of true, responsible and morally preferable actions. By so doing he problematizes the easy equation of true faith (Judaism) with right behaviour and raises the possibility that persons of a heretical tradition might actually be more acceptable to God than those of the traditionally accepted one.

It is of relevance and importance that in Jesus' encounter with people of other faiths, doctrine is not the starting point. Many who have actively engaged in interreligious dialogue confirm that in actual fact discussion of doctrine is the least useful starting point when persons of diverse faith traditions encounter one another. The example of Jesus in this is clear and salutary. Theological (doctrinal) discussion only usefully follows interpersonal empathic interaction that leads to the building of rapport and feelings of common humanity. My intention in discussing these texts here and in engaging students in a classroom setting is that such engagement of scripture is actually pre-interaction, intended for the Christians whose texts are engaged, to help them recognize their own blind spots, in the hope that they might realize that their own foundational texts and founding persons portray a very different attitude to persons of other faiths than the exclusivist and superior attitude adopted by many Christians and churches in their attitudes to persons of other faiths.

Constructive critique of received theologies

It is in this light and with that aim in view that we engage in the next 'movement' in my practical theological cycle – that of a *constructive critique of received theology* from the perspective of the experience, situation and practical engagement with the texts. As for Jesus' encounter with these persons of other traditions, the crucial issue that we critique at this point is the historical and ecclesial tendency not to read these passages as encounters across faiths. Hardly ever do we find commentators emphasizing the 'Roman' centurion's religious background, or the Samaritan's *religious* antagonism to the Jewish faith of Jesus, or else the agricultural and sexual nature of the Canaanite religion to which the Syro-Phoenician woman most likely adhered. We tend to see them as different, but not religiously so. We regard them as 'foreigners', but do not seem to note that they are from *other religious faiths* as well.

The attitude of Jesus also seems to elude us. Each of these persons of other faiths – and there is no textual basis for a belief that they 'became Christians' – is held up as 'having great faith'. With the oppressive Roman centurion Jesus goes as far as to suggest that his faith is greater than all Jews he (Jesus) had met! This is hardly the attitude we find among church people in regard to our Muslim, Hindu, Buddhist or Sikh sisters and brothers to say nothing of practitioners of African religious traditions. Our theology concerning persons of other faiths seems to be informed more by exclusivist interpretations of scriptures or else doctrinal statements intoning the superiority of our faith than by the praxis of Jesus in his interactions with people of other faiths. It would appear rather that experiential learning is a crucial point of departure for relations across faiths.

In Jesus' encounter with the Syro-Phoenician woman, learning takes place across cultures. There is a shared concern for the well-being of the woman's daughter. The desire to restrict the 'good work' of Jesus to his 'own people' alone is challenged and subverted. The most fruitful pedagogical tools and approaches to learning across faiths seems to me to arise out of working together with persons of other faiths on identifiable 'projects' to which we can all be committed. Examples of such work that have been fruitfully engaged in include community organization, community action, care of the homeless, sick and dying; political action for the betterment of our communities; voluntary work – feeding the hungry, providing shelters for the homeless or abused. Chaplaincies – for instance hospital chaplaincies, which have by law had to be multi-faith – have developed much expertise in recognizing, respecting and affirming the faiths of care-recipients, and collaborative work with caregivers from different faith perspectives. Chaplains have often found that drawing on the resources of different faith traditions may enrich and complement deficiencies in any one tradition. The literature, poetry or prayers of different traditions very frequently contain just what is needed to find grace and strength in particular exigencies of life.

Pilgrimages together to sites of historical, cultural and religious significance, especially where interfaith relations are better or else are really challenging, can be the format for reconceptualizing and rethinking one's own attitudes. Organizing for experiential learning through visits to gudwaras, mosques, shrines, temples and other sacred sites is another helpful way to learn. To derive benefit from such visits, though, adequate preparation is called for. Preparation may take the form of training in the pastoral skills of listening, respect, empathy/interpathy, warmth and openness. This is necessary because these visits need to go beyond tourism and begin to lay the foundations for respectful interaction with practitioners of these faiths. Exploring the interaction of gender, race, culture and religion in the social experience of the marginalized and in that of their caregivers can really present opportunities for genuine learning.

A close examination of the praxis of Jesus in interaction with persons of other faiths yields a process that enhances many of the lessons learned by persons who regularly engage in this enriching experience. This realization calls for at least three things, the first of which we have sought to do here: *first*, a re-examination of biblical texts to rediscover and re-unearth interactions and attitudes among practitioners of different faiths, recognizing that the biblical world itself was religiously plural. Especially crucial for Christians is a re-examination of the 'attitude of Jesus' which appears to have been quite different from those of his day, and seems very different from the Church of our day as well. *Second*, a thorough preparation of all who will engage across religious traditions through pastoral skill training; and *third*, engaging experientially with persons of different faiths in community care activities and thus experiencing the joys and frustrations of our common humanity which comprises varied differences including religious ones.

Polyvocal birthday of the Church: The Day of Pentecost

In Acts 2 (Acts 2.1–42), the classic text that describes the founding of the Christian Church, one of the most striking features is the diversity of the languages used by the people upon whom the Holy Spirit came. So diverse are the expressions of praise and thanksgiving from the 120 disciples that the assembled crowd, referred to in the text as 'from every nation under heaven' (v. 5b), are astounded. The bewilderment is declared as lying in the fact that 'each one was hearing them (the gathered followers of Jesus) speak in his own (native) language' (v. 6). In the coming of the Spirit to the Church, God as it were once again announces God's desire for diversity and pluralism in the new creation. The Church as the new creation is intended to declare clearly God's intention for humanity – that we be plural in language, culture and expression of belief. Even where the belief or central affirmation is singular (praise to God), the expression is to be in as many different cultural forms as imaginable. Polyvocality, as expressive of humanity's cultural diversity, is God's chosen means at Pentecost of announcing the inbreaking of the Holy Spirit into the world and the heralding of the new creation (the Church) which is to declare this and embody it to a watching world community. The text takes pains to make clear that this is the work of God, not of humans unaided by the divine. Pentecost is God's declaration and action. At Pentecost God postcolonializes subverting dominant hegemonic discourses and affirms the diversity and plurality of creation. The new creation is to be a postcolonial reality.

2

Postcolonializing God in the USA

Postcolonializing Church and spirituality

I arrived in the USA to live and work in September 2001. Soon after arrival I started worshipping fairly regularly in a Black Church in Atlanta, Georgia. On several occasions I attended worship with a close associate of mine who is also a continental African. After a while, she made it clear to me that she did not feel particularly comfortable with the ethos and worship in this church. I wished to know why. Her response was telling. 'It's just like a session at the traditional fetish shrine back home in my traditional African community', she said. 'When the drumming takes a particularly exuberant form, and they begin to dance, shout and sway, I feel just like I did at the fetish shrine – not at Christian worship. It's just as if the spirits are being invoked and possessions are about to occur – just like the shrine. It's all so pagan and traditional. It transports me back to and re-enacts that from which I thought I had been liberated in Christ!'

What my friend was referring to in 2002, in a telling and remarkable way, is what scholars of Black Religion in the USA have discussed for a long time concerning African roots and retentions within Black Christian spirituality – the 'Africanization' of Black (especially of Slave) Christianity. Was Africa present (as Herskovits argued) or completely erased from Black consciousness (the view articulated by Frazier) in the USA? Is there – and if so in what way is there – an African heritage in Black consciousness? W. E. B. Du Bois, of course, with characteristic insight, preceded the Melville Herskovits/ E. Franklin Frazier debate by many decades. The aspect of Black worship that my associate was specifically disconcerted about,

W. E. B. du Bois (1903) referred to as the 'frenzy' and described it as one of three crucial elements of the Black Church at worship, namely the preacher, the music and the frenzy.[1] Du Bois's description of this aspect of Black worship is worth quoting:

> It varied in expression from the silent rapt countenance or the low murmur and moan to the mad abandon of physical fervor, the stamping, shrieking, and shouting, the rushing to and fro and wild waving of arms, the weeping and laughing, the vision and the trance. All is nothing new in the world, but as old as religion, as Delphi and Endor. And so firm hold did it have on the Negro, that many generations firmly believed that without this visible manifestation of God there could be no true communion with the Invisible.[2]

Du Bois saw this as nothing new in religion but perhaps in his evolutionary sense of religion as present in all early forms. What is interesting is the extent to which for the 'Negro', according to Du Bois, it is such a crucial element of worship that without it there is no true communion with God. The frenzy is as much a theological statement and preference as the sermon or the music. What is intriguing to me is that an unsuspecting continental African in the twenty-first century, exposed to Black worship, is transported into the arena of African traditional religious practice and ritual, experiencing and, in this case, resisting the 'presence of the ancestors' in African American Christianity. This experience raises very serious questions for those who would argue that the African ethos was destroyed and has long lost its real presence in Black Christianity.

Du Bois recognized direct links between the African traditional priest-healer and the Black preacher. He articulated the connection of African American preachers to their African forebears, declaring the priest or medicine man the 'chief remaining institution'

---

[1] W. E. B. Du Bois, *The Souls of Black Folk*, Harmondsworth: Penguin, 1989 [1903], p. 155.
[2] Du Bois, *Souls of Black Folk*, p. 156.

of the African past on plantation life, presenting the scenario of the African traditional priest-healer on the slave plantation thus:

> He early appeared on the plantation and found his function as the healer of the sick, the interpreter of the Unknown, the comforter of the sorrowing, the supernatural avenger of wrong, and the one who rudely but picturesquely expressed the longing, disappointment, and resentment of a stolen and oppressed people. Thus, as bard, physician, judge, and priest, within the narrow limits allowed by the slave system, rose the Negro preacher, and under him the first Afro-American institution, the Negro church.[3]

Levine, Raboteau, Stuckey and many other more recent scholars of Black spirituality, though arguing from different standpoints and often in opposing ways, raise this very issue which lies at the heart of this chapter, namely the connection between African (traditional) religions and Black Christianity in the African Diaspora and the USA in particular.

Sterling Stuckey's carefully researched perspectives on African religion in 'slave culture' are particularly pertinent to this discussion. Stuckey argues that for the slaves 'the retention of important features of the African cultural heritage provided a means by which the new reality could be interpreted and spiritual needs at least partially met'.[4] In other words, for Stuckey, African cultures performed the interpretive and meaning-making function usually attributed to religion for the slave community. The fact that the division between sacred and secular, so prominent in European thinking, was absent in African life and thought resulted in two very different perceptions of African religious cultures. The Europeans despised African religious practices, considering them 'savage, precisely because of its "uniting of seeming opposites"'. For the Africans, on the other hand, 'religion was more encompassing' with, argues Stuckey, 'the ring shout being a principal means by which physical and spiritual,

---

[3] Du Bois, *Souls of Black Folk*, pp. 159–60.
[4] Sterling Stuckey, *Slave Culture*, New York: Oxford University Press, 1987, p. 24.

emotional and rational needs were fulfilled'.[5] It was in fact 'the source of creative genius in the slave community'.[6] Stuckey's insight here is borne out by the sheer number of creative African American impulses and cultural productions whose origins can be traced to African American religion. Says Stuckey,

> Opposition to African religion, therefore, was limited in its effectiveness because the African was thought to have a religion unworthy of the name, when, in fact his religious vision was subtle and complex, responsible for the creation of major – and sacred – artistic forms.[7]

African presence in Black spirituality and the Black Church

The term 'Black Church' is a collective and contested designation for a variety of ways of referring to the African American religious experience in the USA. It may be narrowly defined as a reference only to Protestant Christian and Pentecostal/charismatic denominations and congregations that have been developed and managed by African Americans. Baptist and Methodist denominations of this type are the most numerous. The 'Black Church' is also used to describe Black initiatives within 'mainline' White Christian denominations such as the Roman Catholic, Episcopalian and Presbyterian churches. Moreover, Black Church may be applied to Spiritual and Spiritualist churches established by African Americans. My usage of the term includes these three distinct though at times overlapping phenomena, each of which attempts to respond to the Christian message and categorization. I am using 'Black spirituality' as a way of speaking specifically about the non-Christian religious institutions and forms of practice such as the Islamic, Yoruba and Vodou religious traditions

---

5 Stuckey, *Slave Culture*, p. 24.
6 Stuckey, *Slave Culture*, p. 24.
7 Stuckey, *Slave Culture*, p. 24.

that have come to the USA from the African continent, the Caribbean or South America. Joseph Murphy[8] and Anthony Pinn[9] have both carefully argued and clarified the diversity within the African American religious experience, including its humanist expressions.

Few scholars now would doubt that Africans enslaved in the so-called 'New World' brought aspects of their religious and cultural values along with them and that these had an impact on their lives in many and varied ways. African culture most certainly became part of the amalgam they created that shaped the ethos and culture of nineteenth-century Black life and continued to do so for years after emancipation. Du Bois observed this and stated it with characteristic flourish, utilizing the language of the day and in descriptive, initially disparaging language but which ultimately actually lauds the African past as the reason for the strength and growth of the Negro Church. Reporting in 1903 of the 'Negro church, the first distinctively Negro American social institution', he declared,

> It was not at first by any means a Christian Church, but a mere adaptation of those heathen rites which we roughly designate by the term Obe Worship, or 'Voodooism'. Association and missionary effort soon gave these rites a veneer of Christianity, and gradually, after two centuries, the Church became Christian, with a simple Calvinistic creed, but with many of the old customs still clinging to the services. *It is this historic fact that the Negro Church of to-day bases itself upon the sole surviving social institution of the African fatherland, that accounts for its extraordinary growth and vitality.*[10]

---

8 Joseph M. Murphy, *Working the Spirit: Ceremonies of the African Diaspora*, Boston: Beacon Press, 2003 [1994].

9 Anthony Pinn, *Varieties of African American Religious Experience*, Minneapolis: Fortress Press, 1998.

10 W. E. B. Du Bois (ed.), *The Negro Church*, A reprint of the 1903 edition with an Introduction by Phil Zuckerman, Sandra L. Barnes & Daniel Cady, New York: Alta Mira Press & Rowman & Littlefield, 2003 [1903], p. 5. Italics added.

Du Bois clearly attributed the strength, growth and vitality of the Negro Church to its adherence to the religious heritage of its 'African fatherland'. Stuckey saw Christianity as providing the external form with African ritual being the inner life of the African Church in slavery.

> Christianity provided a protective exterior beneath which more complex, less familiar (to outsiders) religious principles and practices were operative. The very features of Christianity peculiar to slaves were often outward manifestations of deeper African religious concerns, products of a religious outlook toward which the master class might otherwise be hostile. By operating under cover of Christianity, vital aspects of Africanity, which some considered eccentric in movement, sound, and symbolism, could more easily be practiced openly. Slaves therefore had readily available the prospect of practicing, without being scorned, essential features of African faith together with those of the new faith.[11]

Raboteau recognizes religious dynamism and creativity among African Americans in slavery, arguing that

> in the Americas the religions of Africa have not been merely preserved as static 'Africanisms' or as archaic 'retentions'. The fact is that they have continued to develop as living traditions putting down new roots in new soil, bearing new fruit as unique hybrids of American origin. African styles of worship, forms of ritual, systems of belief, and fundamental perspectives have remained vital on this side of the Atlantic, not because they were preserved in a 'pure' orthodoxy but because they were transformed. Adaptability, based upon respect for spiritual power wherever it originated, accounted for the openness of African religions to syncretism with other religious traditions and for the continuity of a distinctively African religious consciousness.[12]

---

11 Stuckey, *Slave Culture*, pp. 35–6.
12 Albert Raboteau, *Slave Religion: The 'Invisible Institution' in the Antebellum South*, New York: Oxford University Press, 1978, pp. 4–5.

Unfortunately Raboteau failed to see the complexity of this African religious consciousness that continued into Black Christianity, suggesting rather naïvely that 'the gods of Africa gave way to the God of Christianity' and that the African heritage may only have influenced the 'spirituals, ring shouts and folk beliefs'.[13] His focus on the Black Church set the tone for studies that excluded the variety of African American religious experience and curtailed a more nuanced study of the complexity of Black Christianity.

Sharla Fett has more recently, with a keener eye for the complexity of African American religious cultures, demonstrated how enslaved women and men on Southern slave plantations drew on African precedents to develop concepts and practices related to health and healing that were distinctly at odds with slaveholders' property concerns.[14] Fett argues convincingly, citing archaeological and other evidence, that Africans enslaved in America embraced a relational view of health intimately related to African religion and community. What is of significance for Black Church and Black Religious Studies is that we are now, perhaps more than at any time in the past, in a position to engage in more careful and informed study of the nature of the influence of African cultural values and non-Christian African religions upon the development of Black life and thought in those harrowing yet formative years. Scholars and students of the Black Church can now study African religions and cultural values more carefully, with a view to gaining insight into aspects of what sustained their forebears who founded the Black Church not only in the expressive and performative forms of culture but also in the nature of belief and the formations of institutional life. In this regard, Black theologians could study the theological implications and significance of African religious concepts and practices in the formative periods of the Black Church and how these worldviews shaped the very nature – and not merely the form –

---

13 Raboteau, *Slave Religion*, p. 92.
14 Sharla Fett, *Working Cures: Healing, Health and Power on Southern Slave Plantations*, Chapel Hill & London: University of North Carolina Press, 2002.

of Black Christianity, making it significantly distinct from White Christianity.

An example of such study is that of womanist theologian Dianne Stewart's work on African religions in Jamaica.[15] Stewart courageously and clearly demonstrates the sustaining power of African religion in the decades before Christianity became a dominant, hegemonic force in Jamaica. She goes on to show the 'indisputable relationship between African religions and African revolts against enslavement'.[16] Stewart argues, on the basis of her close study of Jamaican religious history, that

> if any religious tradition has been a viable force in African liberation struggles in the Caribbean, it is African-derived religion not Christianity. Indeed in those cases where we observe a cohabitation of Christianity with African religion in a single tradition, the evidence demonstrates the primacy of African derived spirituality and religiosity in shaping the identity of the practitioners, even if the practitioners claim to be Christian.[17]

What was true in the Caribbean, as Murphy also shows, was true in North America, where the Black Church incorporated and manifested the power and creativity of Africans enslaved in the USA in initiating religious institutions out of their bringing together of many sources, not least their African religious and cultural worldview. Joseph Murphy studies the services and ceremonies of Haitian Vodou, Brazilian Candomblé, Cuban Santería, Jamaican Revival Zion and the Black Church in the USA – five important traditions of the African diaspora – demonstrating their distinctiveness as well as the similarities among them.[18] 'Each portrait', Murphy indicates, 'has highlighted certain distinctive elements in the "spirit" of each tradition: the revolutionary power of Vodou, the prestige of African precedent in Candomblé, the multiple levels of meaning in

---

15 Dianne M. Stewart, *Three Eyes for the Journey: African Dimensions of the Jamaican Religious Experience*, Oxford: Oxford University Press, 2005.
16 Stewart, *Three Eyes for the Journey*, p. 19.
17 Stewart, *Three Eyes for the Journey*, p. 226.
18 Murphy, *Working the Spirit*, p. 176.

POSTCOLONIALIZING GOD IN THE USA

Santeria, the deliverance from evil in Revival Zion, and the freedom eschatology of the Black Church'. Murphy's rationale for studying these traditions comparatively is instructive: 'Once these elements are seen "side by side", they inform and deepen our understanding of each of the other traditions.'[19] In a similar vein, though with a more pointed appeal, Pinn makes a study of Vodou, Yoruba religion, the Nation of Islam and African American humanism and calls theologians to 'methodical stretching and openness' as they explore 'extrachurch' (the term is Charles Long's) traditions 'as a means by which to understand better the larger complex of African American religious experience'.[20]

Yvonne Chireau, in an illuminating and detailed study of the complexity of African American religious experience and expression, asserts

> Christianity was but one means by which enslaved African Americans interacted with the divine and acquired spiritual empowerment. And while Christianity became perhaps one of the most visible and institutionally viable religions of African Americans, it should be recognized that potential alternatives, including Islam, African-based practices such as voodoo, and other, more discrete religious possibilities such as Conjuring were present in slave communities during the nineteenth century.[21]

Chireau, in discussing supernatural healing beliefs and practices within the Black community, makes the important distinction between the Conjurers, the Pentecostals and the Spiritualists, pointing out, though, that there were clear parallels between them. In studying and assessing this complexity, though, Chireau comes to recognize a common pool from which practitioners of different traditions seemed to draw, asserting that '[p]ractitioners of all three traditions held similar assumptions about the body

---

19 Murphy, *Working the Spirit*, p. 176.
20 Pinn, *Varieties of African American Religious Experience*, p. 5.
21 Yvonne Chireau, *Black Magic: Religion and the African American Conjuring Tradition*, Berkeley: University of California Press, 2003, p. 5.

and embraced analogous visions of misfortune, conceptions of disease, and the uses of spiritual power for extraordinary cures . . . and all drew momentum from cultural sources that had roots in indigenous African spirituality'.[22] As an example, Chireau draws attention to the healing ministry of Bishop C. H. Mason, founder of the largest Black Pentecostal denomination, the Church of God in Christ, who 'owned a collection of unusually formed objects including roots, branches, and vegetables that he consulted as "sources for spiritual revelation" revisiting the tradition of conjuring charms'.[23] It is important to note that in both the practices and the assumptions or structures of belief all drew from the wells of African traditional religious cultures.

Following the recognition and insight of these and several other historians of African American religion and culture, it is possible and I would argue necessary to engage in more close study of the beliefs and practices of the traditional African priest healers to gain a better understanding of one important strand in the development of those early Black preachers. It is possible now to trace more clearly the origins of aspects of the ritual, liturgical and musical traditions of the Black Church as well as the very nature of the belief and doctrinal preferences expressed, for example, in the prosperity gospel, healing, deliverance and spiritual gifts. More careful study can demonstrate the *agency* and the *creative genius* of these largely untutored African Americans. They were sustained by a rich heritage of African values and traditions upon which they drew, mixed creatively with biblical and New World cultural practices into a fascinating tapestry of teaching, worship and church practices. One character in the chapter on 'Herbs and Herb Doctors' in Zora Neale Hurston's *The Sanctified Church*, is Mother Catherine, who 'unlike most religious dictators . . . does not crush the individual.

---

22 Chireau, Black Magic, p. 93.
23 Chireau, Black Magic, p. 113. Mason, as all others in the Pentecostal-Holiness traditions, clearly would disavow any identification with practitioners of Conjure. The point is the phenomenological similarity of his healing and preaching practices with theirs.

She encourages originality.'[24] In Mother Catherine's worship services, 'there is a catholic flavor about the place, but it is certainly not Catholic. She has taken from all the religions she knows anything about any feature that pleases her.'[25] Mother Catherine is the epitome of the creativity of Black religious leaders in the USA. Black theologians need to examine more closely both African religious traditions and contemporary Black liturgical and homiletical practices for their African heritage.

African religious heritage

The main point I am arguing here is that in order to gain a richer sense of the complexity of the nature and texture of Black Christianity and of Black spirituality, a study of African religious, sociocultural and traditional medical and ritual practices (especially as these existed in the seventeenth, eighteenth and nineteenth centuries) is necessary. We must study the presence and impact of the African religious heritage on Black life and thought. Black Christianity, like the other diasporan African religious institutions dubbed 'African-derived religions' in the Caribbean, South and Central America, demonstrates in both belief structure and practice, recognizable traits of African traditional religions. African religions survived and have been recreated in the 'New World' partly because one of the crucial functions of religion in the African mind is to provide the power by which people are enabled to cope with life successfully. The founders and early practitioners of Black Christianity, then, were creative in their formulation of teaching and practice – and they drew on their African religious heritage.

Any careful study of the traditional religious heritage of Africa engages, in my view, *seven* pervasive characteristics which are manifest in different ways among particular peoples and cultures. These

---

24 Zora Neale Hurston, *The Sanctified Church*, New York: Marlowe, 1981, p. 25.
25 Hurston, *Sanctified Church*, p. 26.

characteristics are discernible in African (so called Traditional) Religions on the continent. They are also very much in evidence in the African diasporan religions of the Caribbean, South and Central America which I am collectively calling Black Spirituality. Moreover, and this is the main point of our examining them here, they are abundantly present in the Black Church. Studies of African Independent Churches have not failed to point out how this traditional African worldview is manifest, transposed and operated within these communities of faith. They thus constitute the African religious heritage that is the bedrock out of which all African-derived religious and Black Church traditions are hewn. The seminal characteristics are: (1) the sacredness of all of life; (2) plurality within the divine realm; (3) mystical connectivity through communal ritual; (4) the desire for cosmic harmony; (5) creativity and adaptability; (6) affirmation of life and (7) a pragmatic spirituality.

The sacredness of all of life

It is a commonplace that there are no sharp divisions between the sacred and the secular in African thought. Religion pervades every aspect of life so thoroughly that it is often very hard for the casual observer to recognize its presence let alone distinguish it from culture. Evidence of this lies, on the one hand, in the observation by early European adventurers, such as Rudyard Kipling, that the African has no religion or concept of God; and on the other hand, the pervasive religiosity of Africans everywhere commented upon by various commentators on African social life and picturesquely captured in the note by Kenyan theologian John Mbiti that Africans are 'incurably religious'. The early Europeans were unable to perceive what was woven so closely into the very fabric of African life. Hardly any word exists in most African languages for 'religion' per se. Most often the word 'religion' has been translated by African words for 'ritual' or 'ceremony' or 'service'. The reason lies not in the absence of religion but rather in its pervasiveness. All of life pulsates with the rhythms of the spiritual realm. Mbiti's 'incurably religious' is not to be interpreted in western categories of religiosity divorced from everyday life, or as some narrow innate penchant for superstition, but rather in terms of the pervasive and encompassing zest for life in its multidimensional complexity which often finds expression in very humanistic forms.

Plurality within the spiritual and divine realm

In most of African religious thought the divine realm is populated by many players. Dianne Stewart finds this very evident in the Caribbean and describes it as a 'communotheism'.[26] There is community even in the divine realm. Notions of 'Supremacy' in this realm are often resorted to by many African religious practitioners for the purposes of explanation and translation to the foreign mind, especially the western mind that seems to be so enamoured of counting, measuring and comparing sizes. This point is discussed further in Chapter 4, where the designations of 'polytheism' and 'monotheism' are questioned. The Ultimate Reality (e.g. Akan *Onyame*, Yoruba *Oludomare*, Ibo *Chineke*, Ewe *Mawu*) is so essential and ultimate as to be inaccessible. The Akans say 'If you wish to send a message to Onyame, tell it to the wind.'[27] Onyame is both as close as the air we breathe and as distant as to require a messenger to send requests through. As African sociologist of religion Kofi Asare Opoku has argued, in the spiritual realm there are many different powers – the deities, the spirits, the ancestors and others – which, though distinguishable, constitute collectively the realm of the 'unseen' yet not unexperienced.[28] Reverence is paid to this realm through acknowledgement, prayer in the form of libation, poetry, dance and the music and rhythm of the drum, and other participatory rituals. This plurality is arguably what fuels the deep interest in positive (Holy Spirit) and negative spirits ('Demons') in Black Christianity and in the popularity of 'deliverance ministries' geared towards warding off negative spirits.

---

26 Stewart, *Three Eyes for the Journey*, p. 130.
27 Kwame Gyekye, *African Cultural Values: An Introduction*, Lansing, MI: Sankofa, 1996, p. 9.
28 Kofi Asare Opoku, *West African Traditional Religion*, Singapore: FEP International, 1978.

Mystical connectivity through communal ritual

African religion is not so much a matter of 'beliefs, dogmas and creeds' as it is of the performance of powerful rituals and the expression of communal solidarity through participation in such rituals. There are several rituals that communities, clans and families perform around the *rites de passage* of birth, puberty, marriage and death. There are daily rituals and there are periodic rituals of cleansing, recognition and invocation. Ritual, which is illustrated and discussed further in Chapter 3, is essentially an experience and practice which seeks to foster a deep sense of *belonging* and *participation* in the life of the community and to maintain connectivity with the invisible, mystical realm of existence.

The connection between the visible human realm and the unseen spiritual realm is manifest through that which has been described as 'possession' or 'trance' observable in most African religious ceremonies. Here the plural spiritual realm interacts with the human in ways that incarnate and embody the unseen. Most often such manifestations are ultimately for the good of the human community. Healings, predictions of present and future calamity, proclamations of required ritual performances and indications of the community's need to pursue particular lines of action are some of the results of manifestation of the unseen realm through 'possessions'. The rhythmic language of the drum and the bodily movement of dance are the media through which mystic connectivity is enacted. The language of the drum creates and mediates the liminal space between the visible and the unseen world enabling beings to traverse this space in both directions.

Desire for cosmic harmony

For the human community to flourish, traditional Africans believe that there have to be harmonious relations between the human, spiritual and divine dimensions of existence. A community's ancestors are the mediators of such cosmic relations. Dreams and visions are the regular and normal means of cosmic communication as are 'possessions' and trance states the more formal liturgical or ritual means. To establish this harmony, religious functionaries must both discern sources of disharmony, conflict or destabilization of relations and perform the necessary rituals to correct and maintain good relations. Notions of evil and sin (e.g. *mmusu, bɔne*, Akan) are related to acts and omissions that affect the *sensus communis* of a community.[29] The ritual of libation is the traditional form of prayer believed to mediate this cosmic harmony.

Creativity and adaptability

African religion is demonstrably flexible, pliable, pluralistic and adaptable. The rituals and practices, while maintaining their essential form, have been re-invented in different ways and forms throughout the world. Wherever Africans have gone, willingly or unwillingly, in the world they have formed communities of faith and ritual practice drawing creatively and synthetically on their heritage, as well as upon features of their current context and other realities they have found. The African-derived religions of the Caribbean and South America, the African Independent churches of Africa and Europe, the Black Church of the USA (including the Black Mega-church) are all examples of this African religious creativity. The rhythm, musicality and oral performance of Africans is a combination of this innovativeness, mystical connectivity with the unseen, and the affirmation of embodied life, as is a preference for teaching and doctrine that places the well-being of the human being and community at the centre of spiritual ritual and religious precept.

It is this creativity and adaptability that arguably has sustained and maintained Africans throughout the world in the face of unspeakable and continuous acts of violence and terror directed at them. Evidence of the creative and surviving genius of enslaved Africans lies in the fact that they have managed to incorporate and renovate aspects of their oppressors' religion, transposing it and infusing it with their own latent worldview and culture to

---

29 John S. Pobee, *Toward an African Theology*, Nashville, TN: Abingdon, 1979, p. 111.

the extent that Africa is now spoken of in demographic and geographic terms as within the centre of gravity of Christianity, and the Black Church in the USA is recognized as collectively one of the most vibrant and thriving forms of contemporary Christianity. Amazingly, given the culturally, politically and economically oppressive nature of the transmission of western Christianity in the world and in Africa in particular, Africans, including diasporan Africans, now constitute the largest single racial group practising one form or other of Christianity.

Affirmation of life

The values adumbrated through ritual and practice in African religion are all directed towards the flourishing of human community. Fecundity, bountiful harvests and peaceful communal relations are key prayers in each ritual of libation. Religion is powerfully present through the drum, rhythmic movement of the body and dance not merely through contemplation, reflection or other mental calisthenics. African traditional theology is not only thought out but also expressed in bodily form. Doctrine and ethics revolve around this central thesis, that religious rite and activity needs to promote the well-being of the human community.

Pragmatic spirituality

African traditional spirituality has a pragmatic focus. The most deeply spiritually or religiously adept or developed person is the one who is able to interact with the unseen world in ways that are beneficial to the visible, seen community, especially where ordinary physical and human forces are ineffective. The mark of one's spirituality lies in the ability to help, heal, bless, feed, clothe and shelter the needy through one's efficacious interactions with the unseen realm.

To state that these characteristics of African traditional religions are discernible in African-derived religions in the Caribbean and North America, the African Independent Church Movement in continental Africa, the charismatic church movement, the Black

Church in North America and various forms of Black spirituality is, I suggest, making what is a very obvious observation. To recognize, respect and creatively employ them in the study and practice of Black spirituality and Church is quite another thing, requiring courageous postcolonializing agency.

Black spirituality and the Black Church as New Religious Movements

As briefly mentioned in our consideration of the historical roots of anti-colonialism in Africa, the latter years of the nineteenth and early years of the twentieth century saw the emergence of African Independent (Indigenous or Initiated) churches (AICs) across continental Africa. These AICs generated such interest among scholars of religion as arguably to have spawned the development of the study of New Religious Movements throughout the world.[30] There has been much discussion of the status of AICs – as cults, sects, syncretistic movements, Afro-Christian or authentic expressions of neo-African religions. What is of interest to me is the fact of the development of a whole new interdisciplinary study to approach these religious groups. Spiritual churches (in West Africa) and Ethiopian/Zionist churches (in Southern Africa) have provided the data for many PhD theses. A characteristic feature of these New Religious Movements on the African continent was the creative ability of their founders and leaders to amalgamate African religio-cultural realities with western and eastern beliefs and practices into fascinating syntheses of religious ritual all

---

30 See pioneering studies like Christian G. Baëta, *Prophetism in Ghana: A Study of Some 'Spiritual' Churches*, London: SCM Press, 1962; John D. Y. Peel, *Aladura: A Religious Movement among the Yoruba*, Oxford: Oxford University Press, 1968; Bengt Sundkler, *Bantu Prophets in South Africa*, Oxford: Oxford University Press, 1961 [1948]; Harold Turner, *History of an African Independent Church*, London: Clarendon Press, 1967; and more recently Kwame Bediako, *Christianity in Africa*, Edinburgh: Edinburgh University Press, 1995 and Clifton Clarke, 'Towards an African Post-Missionary Christology among African Indigenous Churches in Ghana', PhD Thesis, University of Birmingham, UK, 2003.

aiming at promoting the healing and wellbeing of devotees. These female and male church founders and prophet-healers were in all the senses we have been discussing exemplars of African postcolonializing activity.

It is my considered view that, taking a cue from the historic studies of 'slave culture' of W. E. B. Du Bois, Sterling Stuckey and others, the Black Church in the USA could be approached along lines in which it is seen as the creation of African prophet-healers who creatively constructed communities of faith, healing and strength out of all the resources that were to hand, including (and by no means solely) from the memories and artefacts of Africa. In another sense the founders and leaders of the Black Church were engaged in postcolonializing activities in the midst of and during the periods of slavery, emancipation, reconstruction, and Jim Crow. Zora Neale Hurston rightly declares,

> if we look at it squarely, the Negro is a very original being. While he lives and moves in the midst of a white civilization, everything he touches is re-interpreted for his own use. He has modified the language, mode of food preparation, practice of medicine, and most certainly the religion of his new country, just as he adapted to suit himself the Sheik haircut made famous by Rudolph Valentino.[31]

To appreciate and positively value the presence of an African religio-cultural underlay in Black Christian spirituality, however, requires us to deal with years of suspicion, fear and downright misinformation concerning non-Christian African faiths. The maligning of these African traditions was a part of the justification of the heinous crime of slavery and the expansion of Europe in its colonialist endeavours. This misinformation set the stage for the continued fear and reluctance to engage in careful study of them especially on the part of continental African scholars. My friend's antipathy towards the 'frenzy' in Black Church worship was informed by this fear, mistrust and misunderstanding.

---

31 Hurston, *Sanctified Church*, p. 58.

It seemed too much like non-Christian African cult practice identified by Mission Christianity as devilish. So in spite of the fairly straightforward Christian content of the service and a strong Pentecostal Christian sermon on discipleship and social holiness with which she would otherwise have been quite at home, the liturgically recognized 'frenzy' in Black Church worship brought up in her the Afro-phobia which is shared by continental and diasporan Africans alike. What is experienced in Black Churches far from being strange or frightening is what theologian Kortright Davis has described as the 'African soul' of Black Christianity, a soul without which there would be little vitality or authenticity.[32]

The initiation and continued progress of the Black Church and of Black spiritual movements lay in the hands of spiritually creative and courageous women and men, descendants of Africa. That creativity is an often ignored characteristic feature of African religions and Black spirituality. Substantial ingenuity is manifest in the development of the Black Church and Black spirituality as manifest in so many African-derived religious institutions. This creativity, which is characteristic of African spirituality, has often fuelled and facilitated an incorporation of 'non-African' phenomena such as western and eastern cultures and practices. Incorporation and inclusivity of varied spiritual entities is a virtue lauded in African traditional religious thought and practice. The African deities are not 'jealous gods'. They recognize power in other beings and are very happy to annex them as allies and to work collaboratively with all. Rather than *analytic* thinking that drives wedges between different parts of a whole, a core aspect of African spirituality is *synthetic* thinking and practice, which incorporates several elements into a 'gestalt' in which the whole always exceeds the sum of the parts.

---

32 Kortright Davis, *Emancipation still Comin': Explorations in Caribbean Emancipatory Theology*, Maryknoll: Orbis, 1982, pp. 50–67, in which he carefully articulates the African foundations of the Caribbean Christian experience.

Historically, in the drive towards legitimization and to gain respectability from the dominant ruling classes and ethnicities in the USA, African sources and resources were driven underground or else into the backrooms of sanctuaries and church structures. Social mobility and assimilation dictated the suppression, at least in public, of practices deemed too 'African' or reminiscent of the ancient despised past. Pentecostal and charismatic renewal in particular, however, gave expression to African spiritual elements, making them more acceptable for the public face of Black Christianity. African religious practices which were the sustaining elements of the slave community prior to emancipation became more permissible when expressed in the forms of Christian worship. I therefore argue that the work of students and scholars of the Black Church and also of Black theologians would be enhanced by more serious and respectful study of their African religious and cultural heritage. Black Church Studies and the broader study of African American religions and spirituality could usefully be seen as studies of global dimensions of African Religion and African Christianity.

In 2004, I led a group of Emory students and alumni on a travel seminar to Ghana. Several fascinating accounts have been and could be shared of the experiences we had on that journey. For several of the participants though, the visit to the churches seems to have been the most disappointing part of their journey to the 'homeland'. They reported that they had expected to find more 'authentic African theology and practice' not the Eurocentric Christianity and versions of the very American 'prosperity gospel' they were treated to. Similarly, for several months an African immigrant church in Atlanta was served by an African American associate pastor ordained within a mainline White US denomination. Although tremendously uplifted by the singing of African songs and the music and rhythm, she reported being struck by the traditionalism and Eurocentricity of the theology of many leaders of the Church. In both these cases, what is striking is the extent to which African Christianity presents itself as authentically Christian by overtly identifying itself with European Christianity.

Continental and diasporan African Christians alike appeal to European scholarship, belief and practice to legitimize their own church practices. Moreover continental as well as diasporan African Christians manifest an antipathy and very often a very deep fear of African religio-cultural beliefs and practices which might appear in their Christian worship or life. Much work, it appears, still needs to be done with both continental and diasporan Africans to help us appreciate the value of African heritage for Christian faith and to move us away from the disdain and antipathy we all still seem to feel towards our African roots.

In approaching African American spirituality in its varied personal, social, institutional and cultural forms, and in the engagement and study of the Black Church as a creative cultural and spiritual institution, I am convinced that there is strong historical continuity and phenomenological similarity between the Black Church in the USA and continental African religious experience and expression and in other African diasporan contexts. As such, I argue that there is much to be gained by approaching the Black Church, historically and contemporaneously, as an expression of African religious creativity and the postcolonializing impulses of Africans influenced by contextual Christianity. To say this is to argue that the Black Church could fruitfully be considered an African religious institution or, more precisely, an African Independent Church (AIC), and as such studied using some of the tools and categories of analysis that have been developed in the study of African Indigenous Churches as 'New Religious Movements'.[33] It is to argue that Black spiritual movements

---

33 These include sermon analysis, cultural analysis, biographical and narrative studies. Harold Turner coined the term 'NRMs' (New Religious Movements) and pioneered many of the methodological studies. Harold Turner is known internationally for his formative contribution to the study of New Religious Movements as a scholarly field. He made his contribution both by extensive field work and by mapping out this new field and formulating the classifications to be adopted within it. The fruits of this work are today housed at Birmingham University, England. An archive of his writings between 1934 and 2002 is available in pdf format on three CD-Roms held at the Henry Martyn Centre, Cambridge, England.

across the diaspora can usefully be recognized historically as New Religious Movements and engaged as such. Both Black spirituality and Black Church then are neither exclusively Christian nor solely African developments. Rather they represent the hybridizing character of all postcolonializing religious movements. Synthetic thinking and dynamic hybrid creativity are hallmarks of such institutions.

I suggest, in conclusion, that comprehensive historical, sociological, psychological, theological and most importantly phenomenological studies of African religious cultures, and the continuities and discontinuities of these in the African diaspora, might open doors to the claiming and linking of heritages and forging of new destinies for people of African descent. Such study could improve the critical quality of scholarship on African religious phenomena across the world, increase our understanding of their complexity, and produce scholars who cannot easily be dismissed as romanticizing and essentializing Africa into a monolithic, mythic colossus impervious to real inquiry. Moreover, this kind of study could provide us with the historical depth and contemporary rigor that is needed in developing the disciplines of Black Church Studies, Black Religious Studies and African and African Diasporan Religious Studies into a robust and invigorating force within seminary and university education facilitating the self-understanding, identity and influence of Black Religious Studies worldwide. This kind of intercultural and interdisciplinary study could offer a more truthful account of the creative agency of all humanity and African people in particular, giving credence to the global nature of African religion, and the postcolonializing genius of the colonized mind.

My call then is for postcolonializing the study of African American religious experience in recognition of the postcolonializing God who has already taken the lead in this activity. Through counter-hegemonic studies that are strategic in addressing the hybridity of Black spirituality and Black Christianity; through interactional and intersubjective studies that allow a large number of authentic voices room to articulate and ritualize their expression; in an ever moving feast of dynamic and creative activities and persons, the rich diversity of the religious experience of persons of African descent can finally find respectable expression.

In the following chapter I present and discuss a liturgical enactment of this postcolonializing ethos, which embodied and portrayed the essence of the desire I am expressing with a very clear aim of re-uniting African communities fractured and kept down by centuries of colonial domination.

3

Postcolonializing Liturgical Practice: Rituals of Remembrance, Cleansing, Healing and Re-connection[1]

Liturgical practice is one of the most visible forms of practical theology. The creation, preparation and practice of ritual are often very significant in the embodiment of religious faith. I have elsewhere written about three kinds of processes that I suggest characterize developments in pastoral care and counselling on the global scene, namely *globalization, internationalization* and *indigenization*.[2] The practice and study of liturgy has followed a similar trajectory. Indigenization, still the least recognized and discussed in the halls of the disciplines of these processes, is occurring increasingly on the ground in very many parts of the world. Models and practices indigenous to non-western contexts which draw on traditional non-western beliefs and practices are being utilized for the 'healing, guiding, sustaining and reconciling of troubled persons'. In this chapter, I would like to present a telling example of the indigenization of practical theology which has clear global import by drawing upon a public ritual that was enacted in Elmina, Ghana in 2007.

---

1 This chapter contains material previously published in an article I contributed to the online *Journal of Pastoral Theology*.

2 See Emmanuel Lartey, 'Globalization, Internationalization and Indigenization of Pastoral Care and Counseling', in Nancy Ramsey (ed.), *Pastoral Care and Counseling: Redefining the Paradigms*, Nashville: Abingdon, 2004, pp. 87–108.

POSTCOLONIALIZING LITURGICAL PRACTICE

An international, trans-historical ritual

On Wednesday 1 August 2007, a ceremony was held on the outer courtyard of Elmina Castle,[3] on the shores of the Atlantic Ocean, at Elmina, Ghana. Under the auspices of the Joseph Project – a program initiated by Jake Obetsebi-Lamptey,[4] then Ghana's Minister (Secretary) of Tourism and Diasporan Relations – the ceremony was advertised as a 'healing ceremony'.[5] What took place that evening was a veritable postcolonial African liturgical and pastoral activity which had been envisaged and crafted and was then conducted as a ritual of remembrance, cleansing, healing and reconnection.

According to the souvenir brochure published by the nation's Ministry (Department) of Tourism and Diasporan Relations to mark Ghana's 50th anniversary of independence and the 200th anniversary of the abolition of the North Atlantic slave trade, 'The Joseph Project is a code name for a series of activities, actions and interactions being spearheaded by Ghana to re-establish the "African Nation" as a nation for all Africans, capable of delivering on the promise of God to Africa and the African people.'[6] Utilizing the image of the biblical Joseph, sold into slavery by his own brothers and then rising to become Chief Minister in the land of his captivity after years of harrowing pain, imprisonment and suffering, the initiators of the project view the relationship

---

3 Elmina Castle, erected by the Portuguese in 1482, as São Jorge da Mina, was the first trading post built by Europeans on the Gulf of Guinea. This edifice is the oldest European building in existence below the Sahara. Established first as a trade post, the castle became one of the largest holding places of Africans to be carried across the Atlantic to be sold into slavery. The Dutch, with the assistance of local Fante people, seized the castle from the Portuguese in 1637. The slave trade continued and was extended by the Dutch until 1814. In 1871 the fort became the property of the British.

4 Son of Emmanuel Odarkwei Obetsebi-Lamptey, one of the founders of the United Gold Coast Convention (UGCC) and one of Ghana's 'Big Six' who led in the struggle for Ghana's independence from Britain.

5 Souvenir Brochure, 'Emancipation Day, Panafest, Joseph Project Launch', *Akwaaba Anyemi*: Golden Jubilee Year 2007, p. 12.

6 Souvenir Brochure, p. 5. The first part of the statement echoes Marcus Garvey's oft repeated slogan 'Africa for the Africans', intended to be a rallying cry of the Back to Africa movement.

between continental and diasporan Africans in terms similar to that of the biblical story. For them the time has come now for the 'Eternal Josephs' to return to their impoverished and famine-ridden home land and be restored to relationship, and themselves also to become agents of restoration to dignity and wealth of a weary continent and devastated people. The 'Purpose' and 'Strategy' statements of Ghana's Joseph Project declare:

> The purpose of the Joseph Project is to make the 21st century the African century – To reconcile and unite the African Peoples so that their positive spirit and strengths are released in a focused manner to elevate Africa and Africans worldwide.[7]

The Project document goes on to say,

> After more than 400 years of slave trading, colonial exploitation, cultural and economic and postcolonial political manipulation much of Africa is a wasteland of woes and war. The African peoples everywhere have been taught to be self-loathing, to see everything African as negative: Taught to believe that Africa is a definition of failure and ugliness. The time has come to put an end to the negative and begin the positive. The time has come for us to till our own vineyard; to produce inner and outer wealth for ourselves. The time has come for us to stand and state, 'I am a proud African, proud of my land, proud of my people, committed to making the third millennium the African millennium.'[8]

The ceremony held on 1 August 2007 was the climax of a series of events heralding the year 2007 – the year of anniversaries – linking and remembering colonialism and slavery, emancipation and independence, liberation and reconciliation and seeking to re-align

---

7 The texts from the ceremony cited in this chapter can be found at Ghana's Joseph Project website www.africa-ata.org/gh9.htm.
8 Souvenir Brochure, p. 5.

African peoples everywhere they find themselves to become connected and to work for a better future for Africans worldwide.

I shall demonstrate that this public ceremony was a postcolonializing, transformative ritual performance with significant practical theological import and implication. That it was organized by a government official and a secular state department rather than by the organized institutional Church is noteworthy and points to the location of significant postcolonializing practical theological activity outside of the walls of the institutional postcolonial Church – an institution which arguably remains stuck with a colonial theology, frozen by the doctrines and practices of its colonialist origins. The postcolonial African Church which exists on the continent as well as in immigrant congregations throughout the world is, as we have already indicated, by and large yet to be truly and fully engaged in 'postcolonializing God'. To a very great extent the postcolonial African Church, especially in its mainline Protestant denominations, simply imitates and regurgitates the theology and practices of her western forebears. This public ceremony in particular, on the other hand, is a significant example of the activities of Africans who are engaged in 'postcolonializing God' through rituals and sacred acts.

To begin with, there are it seems to me *two* central planks upon which the ritual was based. These two are both deeply embedded in African religious thinking and practice. The first central plank of the ceremony, more or less its *raison d'être*, is a core African religious and cultural belief. This understanding, which appears to underlie the whole ceremony significantly, was made explicit in the speeches of both the President of the National House of Chiefs and the Minister of (in US parlance, the Secretary of State for) Tourism and Diasporan Relations. The belief, eloquently expressed symbolically through the rituals, asserts that, analysed from the perspective of African philosophy and spirituality, the economic, political and social privations being suffered in Africa today are not unconnected with the devastations of the heinous trade in African human beings during the sixteenth to nineteenth centuries. A frequently repeated recent example of this way of connecting historic social crime with communal suffering by Ghanaians is the recent military intervention in the political life of the nation of Ghana under Flt Lt (Rtd)

J. J. Rawlings. Many claim that the country's subsequent economic and social woes were in part explainable by the blood that was shed in the heady days of the revolution (dubbed 'house cleaning') unleashed by Rawlings in the 1980s in which many people were summarily executed without due legal process and several suffered beatings, torture and the confiscation of their property. On this view, the degree of devastation in which Africa now lies is in direct proportion to the pain and anguish suffered by the African ancestors kidnapped and transported to serve as slaves in the New World. This linking of past misdeeds to present suffering argues that there can be no real economic, political and social progress on the African continent until this 'social sin' has been atoned for and cleansed. A Ghanaian Christian theologian, John Pobee, helps us understand the breadth of the concept of sin within this African context. 'Sin', he argues, 'is any act, motivation, or conduct which is directed against the *sensus communis*, the social harmony and the personal achievement sanctioned by the traditional code.'9 Pobee further argues that although sins may be committed against an individual or the society in the first instance, Akan society believes them also to be against the ancestors and God. 'For this reason it is believed that the one who neglects to discharge his responsibilities to the less fortunate of the family is punished by the ancestors with some calamity, e.g., death, *saman-yarba* (disease caused by the ghost) and so forth. Therefore in Akan society sin is against the spirit world as well.'10 Thus the *bɔne* ('wicked act' or 'wrong deed' in Akan) of Africa's peoples in the sale of their kinsfolk to the European slavers, similar to the act of Joseph's brothers in selling him to the Midianite tradesmen, is believed to be a direct cause of the current calamitous state of suffering and poverty being endured by Africans on their own continent, which paradoxically is rich in minerals and many other of the earth's resources.

The second has to do with the place and efficacy of *ritual* in African traditional religious life and thought. Ritual is not merely a ceremony

---

9 See John Pobee, *Toward an African Theology*, Nashville, TN: Abingdon, 1979, p. 111.
10 Pobee, *Toward an African Theology*, p. 111.

or activity that one engages in repeatedly as a formalized performance that is symbolic of life's circumstances. To the traditional African mind, ritual is a spiritually powerful means of effecting change in both the *seen* and the *unseen* world. Dr Malidoma Somé, Dagara philosopher and traditional healer, expresses this notion clearly,

> Indigenous [African] people see the physical world as a reflection of a more complex, subtler, and more lasting yet invisible entity called energy. It is as if we are the shadows of a vibrant and endlessly resourceful intelligence dynamically involved in a process of continuous self-creation. Nothing happens here that did not begin in that unseen world. If something in the physical world is experiencing instability, it is because its energetic correspondent has been experiencing instability. The indigenous understanding is that the material and physical problems that a person encounters are important only because they are an energetic message sent to the visible world. *Therefore, people go to that unseen energetic place to try to repair whatever damage or disturbances are being done there, knowing that if things are healed there, things will be healed here.* Ritual is the principal tool used to approach that unseen world in a way that will rearrange the structure of the physical world and bring about material transformation.[11]

Ritual is engaged in to effect transformations in the physical and material circumstances of the living community. Ritual action powerfully changes things. Particularly in respect of healing rituals a significant action has to do with reversals. Through particular rituals curses (ritual pronouncements of ill will) can be *reversed* and transformed into blessings. The ritual activity has to knowingly and symbolically reverse the evil that has been done, spoken or ritually performed. Rituals then are engaged in with the expectation that they will result in transformations on the spiritual plain that will be manifest in the material realm.

---

11 Malidoma Patrice Somé, *The Healing Wisdom of Africa: Finding Life Purpose through Nature, Ritual and Community*, New York: Jeremy P. Tarcher/Putnam, 1998, p. 23. Italics added.

In true African religious form, the 2007 'healing' ceremony drew on customary community (neighbourhood/village/town) gathering protocol, blended with Christian observance and Muslim practice.[12] Aspects of what was done and affirmed would prove offensive to historic missionary and more recent Pentecostal Christian theology. Nevertheless, the rituals of the ceremony demonstrate many hallmarks of a liberative, postcolonializing rite performed with an express aim of reconciling communities of African descent, healing of relationships and cleansing a people of the spiritual and material contaminations of heinous crimes against humanity.

To appreciate and discuss the nature of the ceremony and its postcolonializing efficacy, let us now examine it closely in the order in which the rituals unfolded.

Opening ceremonials

The ceremony opened with the playing of traditional ceremonial drums. The beating of these types of drums traditionally is the means of summoning all and sundry to a solemn, auspicious and very important community meeting. The type of drum together with the language of the drum is understood by traditional people as a summons to a solemn ceremony. In response to the summons of the drums, the gathering assembly was 'called to order' by the entrance of the chiefs and traditional rulers of the Cape Coast and Elmina traditional areas in palanquins and all the paraphernalia of Ghanaian traditional chieftaincy. They, along with chiefs and traditional rulers from other parts of the region and country, entered the prepared grounds and into the durbar of the community amid the firing of musketry, with the traditional drum language moving on to announce the start of a great and solemn assembly of all people for a sacred and highly significant communal activity. The regalia, traditional ceremonial attire and movement onto the

---

[12] African religious traditions are synthetic rather than analytical. It is an African religious virtue for practitioners to blend together many different practices and beliefs. The ability to incorporate and include different spiritual entities from different sources is lauded.

durbar grounds of the chiefs all bespoke the nature of the ceremony and its significance for the well-being of the people. In the assembly, seated under canopies some of which bore labels indicating where they had come from, were people from many different African and Caribbean countries as well as from Europe and North America. A group of 28 of us had travelled to Ghana from the USA under the auspices of Candler School of Theology's Black Church Studies Program and participated fully in the proceedings.[13] Jake Obetsebi-Lamptey's envisioning statement for the ceremony was that it would

> assemble the traditional rulers of those tribes that engaged in the Atlantic slave trade from across the West and Central Coast of Africa: the traditional rulers of those tribes whose people still have living memory of being hunted by slave raiders; and recognized leaders of and the Africans in the Diaspora.

The chiefs and traditional rulers present stood in for and served as representatives of all the 'tribes that engaged in the Atlantic Slave Trade'. Chiefs and traditional rulers across West Africa recognize their representative functions and often symbolize this through their linguists (spokespersons) and the staves of office that are carried ahead of them in processions. These carvings of various symbols and creatures are insignias, emblems or totem animals of various communities. The staves and emblems of office speak of the communities they represent and thus symbolically indicate the presence of many who may not be physically present.

Re-entry through the 'door of return'

Following the entrance of the traditional rulers, the Master of Ceremonies (MC, as named on the printed programme), who for my purposes is best described as 'liturgist', made an announcement

---

[13] The group was led by Dr Alton B. Pollard, then Director of Candler's Black Church Studies Program, and myself.

inviting diasporan Africans to enter the sacred grounds through a replica door. A replica door made of wood, with the words *Door of Return* emblazoned clearly in black and gold letters upon it, had been erected on the grounds.[14] All diasporan Africans present were invited to process through this 'door of return', symbolically reversing the harrowing exit of their ancestors through the 'door of no return' in the dungeons below the castle. Diasporan Africans from North America, Europe, the Caribbean and elsewhere then marched in single file through the replica door onto the courtyard and into the ritual space that had been created by the positioning of the seating canopies and the dais erected for the officiating dignitaries and special guests.

A highly significant aspect of the location of the replica door was that it had been erected and placed on top of a compass carved into the stone of the courtyard by the Portuguese in the fifteenth century. The compass had served both as a position marking and a time keeping device. Thus this procession served symbolically to reverse both in terms of location and time, the journey centuries before of the captured Africans. The symbolic reversal was thus both spatial and temporal. The descendants of the enslaved symbolically and ritually reversed the time by walking backwards over the colonizers' timepiece. They also reversed the location by symbolically and ritually marching through the replica door erected outside, freely turning the 'door of no return' (through which the ancestors had passed on the harrowing journey from freedom onto the slave ships that carried them away) into a 'door of return' through which they symbolically returned through their descendants to their long lost homeland. The ritual procession ushered the daughters and sons of the enslaved back in time and space and then on into the future as returned exiles to their African homeland. Obetsebi-Lamptey expressed the ritual significance of this procession in the following cryptic way: 'They

---

14 A wooden replica of the 'door of no return', which European slavers had constructed in the castle, and through which their ancestors had passed centuries before onto small canoes that carried them to the waiting slave ships.

will reverse the Journey that started four hundred years ago with the "Door of no Return".'

Introit: Music from the Afro-beat virtuoso band Osibisa[15]

As an 'introit' to accompany the re-entry of the diasporan Africans and to express the desire of their hosts to receive them and the ancestors back to their homeland, the song *Welcome Home*, composed by the Afro-beat group Osibisa in 1975, was rendered live by the celebrated band at this point. *Welcome Home* declares the proverbial Akan *Akwaaba* (an Akan word meaning 'welcome') not merely to the ceremony but more so as an embrace by the local people of the descendants of those who had been forcibly removed centuries before. To the sounds of drums, guitars, saxophone, flute, trumpet and keyboards, the Afro-beat band sang:

> You've been gone for far too long; you've been gone – it's an empty home,
> Come on back where you really belong, you are always welcome home, welcome home.
> You've been kept down for much too long, stand up please and say 'I am free', don't forget you are always welcome home.
>
> (*Refrain*)
> Come with me on this happy trip back to the promised land. All will be happy and gay.

---

15 Founded in London by four Africans and three Caribbean musicians in 1969, Osibisa played a central role in developing an awareness of African music among European and North American audiences in the 1970s. Founding members included Ghanaians Teddy Osei (saxophone), Sol Amarfio (drums) and Mac Tontoh (trumpet), Nigerian Lasisi Amao (percussion and tenor saxophone), and Grenadian Spartacus R. (bass), Trinidadian Robert Bailey (keyboard) and Antiguan Wendell Richardson (lead guitar). Their extremely danceable sound is an energetic and polyrhythmic blend of African, Caribbean, Jazz, Blues, calypso, Latin, R & B and Funk-rock. Band members use the name Osibisa to mean 'crisscross rhythms that explode with happiness'.

Come on back, to where you really belong, welcome home; don't forget you are always welcome home.

As an invitation, invocation and a statement of purpose no piece of music could have been more appropriate for this occasion. No other lyrics could perhaps convey the high emotion and feelings of loss and return palpable in the music. Pastorally this introit deeply communicated to the assembly the meaning and significance of the ceremony. Further, it set the scene musically and in mood for what was to follow.

Cleansing: A ram for sacrifice

For a rite of pacification to be performed a spotless white ram was carried at this point on the shoulders of a bare-chested man to a central point of the courtyard and the sacred gathered assembly. Animal sacrifice has been a long standing aspect of different religious traditions including Judaism. African religious traditions continue this practice which symbolically provides a decisive and noteworthy act through which the taking away of guilt and sin may be symbolically recognized. The size of the sacrificial animal is culturally commensurate with the gravity of the offence. On occasions where a great and terrible misdeed is to be atoned for, an unblemished white ram symbolized the shedding of blood for the expiation of the sins of the whole people. This is also a rite of pacification in recognition of the gravity of the evil done.[16] In conceptualizing the ceremony Obetsebi-Lamptey had written,

> There will be expiation, based on the recognition that great evil was done by those who traded in their kith and kin, by those

---

16 The white ram was carried on the shoulders of traditional religionists onto the centre court of the grounds and presented to the chiefs and priests. The officiants and traditional priests acknowledged the ram and directed that the actual slaying take place somewhere other than the grounds – in the privacy of a sacred shrine room. Invited dignitaries would partake of the meal prepared from this sacrifice later that evening.

in the Homeland for whom the memory of being hunted is still alive and by the ancestors of those who were forced into the agonies of the middle passage and chattel slavery.

Invocation and prayers by religious leaders

At this point prayers were offered. A significant feature within this liturgy was the coming before God of leading representatives of the three demographically largest faith groups in the country – Christian, Muslim and African Traditional Religion. Obetsebi-Lamptey's vision in calling for prayers was that 'this "Healing" will be in both modern religious and traditional forms' and would be a 'ceremony of rapprochement in traditional and multi faith forms'. On this occasion it was clear in the prayers of Christian, Muslim and Indigenous religionist that each recognized a great evil had been perpetrated against the people and what was being sought through prayer was forgiveness, healing and reconciliation. Each religious leader made reference in their prayers to their respective sacred texts (written and oral) in seeking divine wellbeing for all the descendants of those who had been involved in the heinous trade. The traditional priest engaged in the prayer ritual of libation.

The pouring of libation is the rite of prayer and invocation within most African religious traditions. It is also one of the most contested of traditional African religious practices conceived by missionary Christianity as the invocation of other 'gods' and even 'demons'. An analysis of traditional libation texts bears testimony to the fact that the Creator is always the first mentioned and invoked. Other forces are recognized, including the ancestors and spiritual forces both good and evil. However, blessing is sought for the community from all 'good forces'. Like the psalmists often did, those fomenting or desiring evil for the community are rebuked. There is never an invocation of evil against any who seek the wellbeing of the gathered community. Following a critical study of the subject, Ghanaian Christian theologian John Pobee comes to the following conclusion:

We believe that if the content of the prayers could be made consonant with Christian theology, libation could be incorporated into Christian worship. But as it happened, the Christian church rejected libation outright.[17]

Because it remains a contested ritual, libation as prayer is discussed again in Chapter 5 of this book. The rejection and disparaging of this form of prayer represents an example of the destruction of a people's rich culture through ignorance by colonialists whose fear, misapprehension and misinterpretation has been introjected by local Christians who today continue to fear and misconstrue this form of prayer in ways that practitioners of the religion out of which it comes never did. Pobee's suggestion, if it had been accepted and implemented, would have been a tremendously evocative postcolonializing act through which a rich cultural and religious tradition of the colonized could have become a vehicle of great significance in the portrayal of faith.

Greetings and salutations: The recognition of the 'Eternal Josephs'

Present at this ceremony were three significant African diasporan representatives dubbed 'eternal Josephs' by Obetsebi-Lamptey. Dr Joseph Garvey (son of Marcus Mosiah Garvey), Rita Marley, (wife of the legendary musician Bob Marley) and a great grand-niece of African American abolitionist, freedom fighter and 'conductor' of the Underground Railroad, Harriet Tubman, were at this point in the proceedings introduced to the gathering and together moved around the grounds greeting and being acknowledged by the crowd. Following these official ceremonial representatives, people of African descent from countries in Europe and the Caribbean were also introduced to the gathering and brought greetings.

---

17 Pobee, *Toward an African Theology*, p. 65.

Choral music by the Winneba Youth Choir[18]

One of Ghana's most versatile interdenominational church youth choirs rendered a selection of Ghanaian composed choral music. Apart from the Christian prayers, this was the only part of the ceremony where overtly Christian language and idiom was on display. The fact that the music itself was choral in a western sense was not obscured but the nature of the compositions and the language of the lyrics were African. This in itself was an important postcolonializing feature. African composers utilized a western musical form and performative structure transposing it by their own composition and language and then rendering the production to reverse and as it were overturn the work of the colonizers.

Confession and request for pardon

The President of the Ghanaian National House of Chiefs at this juncture offered an unreserved apology for the part the predecessors of all African traditional rulers and chiefs played in the iniquitous trade in human beings. In his speech, he asserted without equivocation that 'the chattel trade in human beings was totally indefensible, immoral, and inhuman and that the participants, both African and non-African, stand condemned'.[19] He refused to exonerate any who lived at the time, asserting that 'ignorance is no excuse'. Rather he prayed that all who learn of this inhumanity should resolve, in the words of the National House of Chiefs,

---

18 The Winneba Youth Choir was founded in May 1989, under the direction of George Mensah-Essilfie. It is interdenominational and is made up of young people between the ages of 10 and 20 years. The choir seeks to project a positive image of African youth and African choral music.

19 Drolor Bosso Adamtey I, Suapolor Se State, 'The Trans-Atlantic Slave Trade 1500–1800s AD: We were all involved', in James K. Anquandah, *The Trans Atlantic Slave Trade: Landmarks, Legacies, Expectations* (Proceedings of the International Conference on Historic Slave Routes held in Accra, Ghana, 30th August–2nd September, 2004), Accra, Ghana: Sub-Saharan Publishers, 2007, p. 18.

In everlasting memory of the anguish of our ancestors.
May those who died, rest in peace.
May those who return, find their roots.
May humanity never again perpetuate such injustice against humanity.
We the living vow to uphold this.[20]

Obetsebi-Lamptey writes: 'Without knowledge and understanding there can be no genuine reconciliation. Without reconciliation there can be no forward movement.'

The declaration of guilt was without equivocation, the prayer for pardon was direct and the resolution to work to ensure that such inhumanity was never again repeated was fulsome. This act of confession bore all the signs and elements required of repentance. The declaration was followed immediately by one of the most significant and emotionally charged aspects of the whole ceremony.

The washing of the hands of diasporan Africans by the traditional rulers

By far the most moving act of the ceremony, a multivalent activity which symbolized remembrance, cleansing, healing and reconnection all at once, occurred when the traditional rulers moved out of their seats, in direct contravention of traditional African protocol for chiefs, to bowls and basins that had been placed centrally on the grounds. They invited diasporan Africans from all over the world to come forward to the bowls and proceeded to wash their hands in the water in the bowls, in which hyssop plants had been placed. In the Bible, hyssop has been associated with cleansing.[21] The power of the symbolic action of the chiefs, many of whose predecessors had engaged in the sale of their ancestors, washing the hands of the descendants of slaves and asking their pardon evoked many

---

20 Plaque on the front wall of the male slave dungeon of the Cape Coast castle, Cape Coast, Ghana.
21 See for example Exodus 12.21–4; Leviticus 14.1–4, 33–49; Numbers 19.1–10; Psalm 51.7.

overwhelming feelings. The sacred symbolism of the act was both evocative and inspiring. Pardon was then sought through word – open verbal acknowledgement, confession, and request for forgiveness. It was also sought through deed – the symbolic washing of the hands of the descendants of those wronged. It was the traditional rulers whose predecessors had been brokers in the iniquitous trade who initiated the act, symbolizing their desire for pardon and cleansing of the victims of their predecessors' misdoings.

Traditional rulers, when sitting publicly in court, do not ever rise from their official seats to perform any tasks. Nor do they ever perform any menial tasks such as washing the hands or feet of guests. These roles are reserved for servants of the royal court. In spite of this customary etiquette, in this solemn ceremony the chiefs themselves agreed to reverse their role and protocol in order that the ritual symbolism would be very plain and effective in both public and ancestral realms. It is striking that traditional rulers, practitioners of African religions, proved to be more willing to demonstrate public contrition and to break with protocol in their spiritual quest for healing and well-being in world community than many Christian and Islamic leaders have shown themselves to be. The practitioners and public custodians of traditional African religion showed incredible flexibility, adaptability and ethical responsibility in this matter.

Sermons: Addresses from the minister and other guests

The Minister (Secretary) of State in his address highlighted the importance of the 'rapprochement of the African peoples'. Obetsebi-Lamptey emphasized that 'there can be no African century without unity of the African peoples'. In line with African traditional belief and theology, the constraint to unity, he argued, lies in the 'restlessness of the spirits of our ancestors'. 'Unatoned violence leaves the spirit disturbed; the 300 years of the slave trade and the years of slavery and subjugation that followed, subjugation that has yet to end, have been years of violence to our people. We must lay the spirits to rest.'

Obetsebi-Lamptey clearly envisaged this ceremony of healing as a beginning of a process of reconciliation and rapprochement between African 'homelanders' and 'diasporans'. He went on to say,

> We cannot but be aware of the real bitterness felt by many of our brothers and sisters in the diaspora against those of us still in the homeland. However, it is important that those outside realize that their pain is shared by many brother and sister Africans still in Africa: For every son who went out to play and never returned and who grieves till today, there are the parents still lamenting their son who disappeared; for every mother who disappeared when out gathering firewood, there are the motherless infants; for every father who left to go hunting, there is the fatherless family.

Obetsebi-Lamptey recognized the need for education, lest we forget and lose sight of the need for vigilance in the struggle for humanity for all.

> What happened during these 400 years must never be forgotten. Already there are signs of a growing amnesia about the slave trade in the homeland. The young, and not so young, in the diaspora are also showing a lack of interest in knowledge of that terrible period.

The vision of the framers of this ceremony and the symbolic rituals they crafted were not exclusively negative. The ceremony was not merely symbolic as in the rite of hand-washing, a positive social, political and international outcome was envisaged. Obetsebi-Lamptey, perhaps in political hyperbole, declared,

> While we lament over the wickedness of the Slave Trade we must not lose sight of the display of greatness of the African spirit that it showed. Our people were in bondage in the land of the oppressor, chattel slaves, yet they turned round to dominate their oppressors so that, today, African culture, African language, African music dominates world culture, world language, world

music. The strength of this spirit is epitomized by those Africans in the diaspora who rose and continue to rise far above their chains to attain and display excellence.

As a monument to the human capacity to transform the tragic into the triumphant, the Minister declared his then government's intention,

> to convert one of the slave forts, James Fort in Accra, a fort that kept first slaves and then prisoners, a true example of the attempt to chain mankind, into the home of the African Excellence Experience. We will build in this slave fort, from which our peoples were shipped out supposedly never to return, a museum dedicated to those Africans in all walks of life who triumphed over slavery, who triumphed over every adversity; who triumphed and continue to triumph over those who sought to enchain them: – we will build a monument to The True Josephs. In this fort we will mount a state of the art exhibition of the slave trade; from hunting captives, through the march to the coast, the middle passage and onto the plantations of the Americas and to the continuing struggle for civil rights.
>
> At this monument you will relive the story of Mary MacLeod Bethune, Frederick Douglas, Harriet Tubman, Marcus Garvey, Toussaint L'Ouverture, Duke Ellington, Martin Luther King, George Washington Carver et al.
>
> We will tell not only the story of the gross inhumanity but we will also tell the stories of the continual struggle for freedom and against the imposition of the yoke. We will tell the story of Toussaint L'Ouverture, the Maroon revolts, the refusal by so many of our people to accept the shackles of those who have sought and continue to seek to subjugate us.
>
> Having passed through this exhibition you will then enter the cells and dungeons of the slave fort/prison and here we will exhibit the life stories of the 'Josephs'. Those who triumphed

over the extreme adversity of the slave trade, its aftermath and consequences and triumphed in all areas of human endeavour. All the 'Josephs' of blessed memory and you will also meet the Josephs of today, those still alive, whose lives are an inspiration to us, whose lives are blazing torches of the true African spirit.

The overall aim, motivation, desire and message of the ceremony is articulated thus:

> An African, whether homelander or diasporan, visiting this experience should emerge strengthened, better able to overcome whatever challenges he or she may face through the examples of the 'Josephs'. Truly it will show that the African spirit can never be chained. Here in the 'African Excellence Experience' we will find the inspiration to overcome all of life's challenges. Here we will share the strength and power and inspiration of those who rose and triumphed and continue to triumph over the greatest of all adversities.

Other invited guests, including representatives from neighbouring West African countries, also gave short addresses calling on the living to ensure that they rise above the horrors of the past, forge a united and courageous front and arise to overcome whatever challenges Africans face the world over.

Closing: Celebration of the new African in the world

Obestebi-Lamptey envisaged 'a concert of praise that will signal the new beginning, to right a terrible wrong, to get good out of bad'.

The ceremony ended with celebration, drumming, dancing and jubilation to the music of Osibisa. Rulers, people, chiefs and members of their communities, African peoples from Europe, North America, the Caribbean and all gathered celebrated together through dance and movement. All the rituals of remembrance, cleansing, healing and reconnection were taken up in this closing act of celebration. In African religious jubilatory fashion spiritual experience was expressed through bodily movement. The whole of a person – not merely the mind, voice or spirit – was used in praise of God and embodiment of new hopes and aspirations.

Postcolonial practical theological reflection

My reflections on the postcolonializing nature of this ceremony will be presented under the headings of the seven characteristics of postcolonializing activities enumerated in the first chapter.

First, the ceremony had *counter-hegemonic*, insurgent and subversive features. Although initiated by a government official, it challenged the silence of previous governments, the educational system inherited from the colonialists which largely overlooked any teaching of the subject of slavery, the traditional culture of silence over slavery[22] and the collusion of the Church – both missionary and postcolonial – in the failure to face head on the realities and effects of slavery. This ceremony turned the 'culture of silence' on its head and not only spoke directly to it, but also faced up to historic local culpability, devised powerful symbolic rituals of reversal – such as the 'door of return' – and sought atonement, cleansing and redirection of energy from the horrors of the past.

Second, this ritual as an example of African theology in practice was *strategic* and transformative in intention and action. It ritualized the African traditional belief that conditions in the physical, material world often reflect spiritual conditions from the past or present. Rather than ignore or suppress this belief (as mere superstition) the crafters of the rite incorporated it into 'word and

---

22 Wilhelmina J. Donkoh, 'Legacies of the Trans Atlantic Slave Trade in Ghana: Definitions, understandings and perceptions', in James K. Anquandah (ed.), *The Trans Atlantic Slave Trade: Landmarks, Legacies, Expectations* (Proceedings of the International Conference on Historic Slave Routes held in Accra, Ghana, 30th August–2nd September, 2004), Accra, Ghana: Sub-Saharan Publishers, 2007, pp. 305–23, shows how local taboos and fear of stigmatization associated with slavery and slave origins have resulted in lacunae in available histories. Her paper provides documentation of oral accounts of real life experiences and family traditions handed down to descendants of 'slavers' and 'slaves' who never crossed the Atlantic.

symbol'. The desire to effect change in the social realm through recognizing the social and economic effects of *mmbusu* ('unspeakable social sin' in the Akan language) points to an endorsement of a deeply felt African religious sentiment which in point of fact exists also in other cultures and faiths. The ritual acts of cleansing, washing and confession are seen to have salvific effects within the living community – the transformation of communal suffering into material well-being. The strong belief in the efficacy of communal ritual in reversing material conditions is affirmed through tangible practices.

Ancestors, in African life and thought, are perceived as the arbiters of the moral life of the community. So when it is the ancestors themselves who have been grievously wronged you have a recipe for chaos and disaster in the living community. This fundamentally is the problem with the living African community, viewed through the lenses of an African theology and spirituality. The ancestors suffered traumatic dislocation from their natural environment, being ripped from their human communities. Dislocated, disgraced, degraded and desecrated in life, they were not laid to rest in ceremonially and traditionally fitting burials. Unatoned-for violence, economic and material dislocation stalks the land of the living, because the ancestors (the judges) were themselves violently violated. Until this condition is ritually and spiritually addressed there will continue to be chaos within the living community. The ceremony then was designed and enacted to reverse, atone for, cleanse and transform the whole of the African community, living or dead, and so to usher in a renewed African community throughout the world. This ceremony served as an 'organic' act uniting theory (belief) with action in efficacious sacred ritual.

The ceremony was markedly intentional. Its planning and execution were highly commendable. Thoughtful planning and careful execution spoke of the carrying out of a strategic vision for a better experience for people of African origin worldwide. It clearly portrayed the vision encapsulated in the 'Joseph Project' first articulated several years before the actual event. The representation of the 'eternal Josephs' was clearly intended to signal the breadth and variety of the African diasporan family and to indicate just how vast a resource that is for the uplifting of Africa as a human community rather than merely a geographical location.

Another aspect of the strategic intent of the ceremony cannot be overlooked. This was a purposeful, political and economic event. Not only did it deal symbolically and ritually with the ghosts of the past, it also served to inspire and give some direction to present-day living Africans. It pointed to possibilities of a renewed relationship between continental Africans, diasporan Africans as well as Europeans and Americans of European origin. One need not ignore the boosting of the 'tourism' industry on the West African coast – a source of much needed revenue for the countries of the former 'Slave and Guinea' coasts – nor deny the possibilities for new trade and commercial links with Europe and America that may properly reverse the revenue flow which has been unidirectional since even before the inception of the Transatlantic slave trade.

Third, there is a *hybridity* and 'messiness' which is both unsystematic and interreligious about the postcolonial practical theology in evidence in this ceremony. The rituals engaged in sought to bring a divided people into mutual engagement and 'agreement' (reconciliation) rather than to invoke concrete 'successes'. How does one deal systematically with such a painful, historically fraught issue as the sale and traffic in 'one's own kith and kin', collusion with the oppressor, and the manifest guilt and inhumanity of 'respectable' persons such as a community's royals? The rituals engaged in attempted to encase the mess in symbolic inter-subjective practices that pointed towards other ways of being in the world. Participants had to become involved in the messiness of historical action. There could be no 'objective' onlookers. All, whether oppressed or oppressor, played a part in what happened then and as such need to be a part now in the symbolic act of reversal.

A significant aspect of the hybridity of the ceremony was that it was ecumenical in a very wide sense, including practitioners and rituals from three faith traditions. Missionary and postcolonial Christianity in Africa has repeatedly been unable to ritually engage with traditional African beliefs and practices in ways other than characterizing these beliefs and practices in pejorative terms. European pagan practices have relatively easily found their way into Christian rituals. African traditional practices such as Libation, which arguably have many points of contact with Judaeo-Christian beliefs, have constantly been denigrated and demonized. 'Fear of evil' has been the major obstacle to the embracing of African traditional practices. African and non-African Christians have been very reluctant to recognize African religious practices as permissible in the daylight of ritual activities. The heart of libation is an honouring of one's ancestors. The traditional belief structure encompassed by the rite of libation is essentially this: 'Honour your father and your mother, that your days may be long in the land that the LORD your God is giving you' (Exod. 20.12).

This ceremony lifted up plurality as normative and allowed practitioners of different religious faiths to pray alongside each other. Admittedly, this happens routinely at state functions, in respect of a national political structure that declares itself secular and plural.

Nevertheless, this ceremony was not strictly speaking a 'state' function. It might be described as a semi-formal or inter-communal activity. The fact that it was so 'religious' in character might have suggested institutional religious origins. It seemed like an 'unofficial state religious rite of atonement and reconciliation with ancestors'. The liturgist (or MC) Fritz Baffuor was a local Member of Parliament with no formal religious training. The rituals encompassed western Christian, Muslim and traditional African religious rites and ceremonials – some of which have historically been highly antagonistic towards each other – clearly demonstrating the hybridity of the postcolonializing rite and the plurality of religious traditions embraced in its ecumenicity. Two adjectives capture the ceremony significantly – namely 'ancestral' and 'spiritual'. It took ancestors seriously both in their suffering (those captured) and their culpability (those who colluded with the slavers). The living rulers recognized that their noble ancestors were also culpable. They engaged in a spiritual rite that sought to transcend time and transform space. For cleansing to occur of such historic wrongdoing it was necessary for both time and space to be transfigured.

Fourth, the *interactional* nature of the ritual was evidenced in the many opportunities given for persons of African origin domiciled in different parts of the world to meet up. The climactic event of the hand-washing by the traditional rulers was perhaps the highest point in the ceremony. It was also the most interactional. The interaction was at many different levels. There was that actual real time touching of a current continental African communal leader with an American, European or Caribbean person – present-day African royals meeting today's generation of diasporan African commoners. Then there was the ancestral 'touching' of a descendant of likely colluders and participants in the heinous trade, with descendants of those so traded. Moreover, there was the interfaith interaction between practitioners of African religions, overt western and African Christians and Muslims, persons of Christian or Muslim faith who in belief and practice, often in times of crisis, is manifestly traditional African. This is to say nothing of age, gender, class, ethnicity and sexual orientation, among other features of the diversity that was present among participants in the ceremony. This was symbolic interactionalism of a high order.

Fifth, the ceremony was a *dynamic* expression of faith in action. Osibisa's selections were from past and present portions of their long and varied repertoire. The Winneba Youth Choir rendered pieces from recent choral compositions of Ghanaian and European origin. Both music groups gave expression to the desire for past and present to cohere in ways that could and would move things along. We cannot nor should we deny or cover up the past. But neither should we be defined by it. In line with the Akan symbol and word '*sankofa*', the past needs to be learned from for the present and the future to be different.

Sixth, the ceremony was *polyvocal.* Voices from the past and the present were heard. Voices from Europe, the Caribbean, the Americas, the African continent in varying stages of migration and transition all found expression in the ceremony. Many sometimes contradictory voices were heard. There was no attempt to smooth things over or to harmonize them in artificial ways. The voice of the waves of the Atlantic Ocean beating on the crisp sand on the shores was not silent but rather seemed to echo with the cadences of the voices of ancestors long dead.

Seventh, the ceremony is an example and telling illustration of a significantly *creative* ritual activity in which all persons could participate and from which all could receive instruction as well as inspiration. The crafters employed incredible ingenuity in creating transformative symbols, such as the construction and placing of a 'door of return', the washing of the hands of the descendants of the victims of the crime by the descendants of those who colluded in its perpetration in water garnished with the cleansing power of hyssop, the choice of the introit 'Welcome home', the invitation and inclusion in the programme of the 'eternal Josephs'. In these and other ways the creativity of a people free to draw on their religious culture in the creation of ritual is laudatory.

Conclusion

A deeply pastoral postcolonializing activity took place on 1 August 2007 at Elmina, encompassing individual and interpersonal as well as global pastoral care – healing of memories and of ongoing pathologies; reconciliation of communities long taught to hate each other; guiding generations of youth into the ways of justice and peace; sustaining persons who had lost hope that there would ever be an acknowledgement and repentance for crimes against humanity. The ceremony enacted in a specific space/time location powerfully ritualized a much needed global *remembering*, calling a traumatic past into a conscious redemptive present; *cleansing*, through the symbols of water and hyssop and the action of washing by representatives of the guilty of representatives of the victims; *healing*, ushering in a new era of emotional wellness, repairing legacies of disease; *re-connecting*, bringing fractured communities into touch with each other again.

Many of the African American participants commented significantly on the transformative, life-giving and personal empowering effects of the ceremony for them. An example is that of an African American clergywoman member of our travel group who wrote the following words in reflection on the momentous occasion:

> 'Remembrance' (Re-member-ance) that's what this reconciliation ceremony spoke to me. Images continue to flood my head and heart each time I tell and re-tell the story of one of the greatest and most significant experiences of my life. Sitting in the strength of the sun-kissed rays, my ears are attentive to the sounds of the calling to my heart. It is the voices in the roaring ocean waves that seem to speak to me in a calming, comforting yet urgent way and the song of Osibisa 'Welcome Home' reached deep to my soul serenading my heart and re-connecting, re-membering my ancestral self . . . and it was then! That was the moment that I REMEMBERED . . . My spirit-woman leaped! Yes, I remember now it was right at that very moment in time as we sat on the grounds outside of Elmina Castle. My eyes captive as they soaked up the magnificent canvas of bright colours and beautiful people . . . my people. I knew that I knew, something great, something huge, and something that was always there buried in the separation and laying at the bottom of the Atlantic Ocean with all those who were cast to the endless myrrh, and this was the point where it all took place. I knew without a doubt that I had truly come home. My hands were washed in hyssop and this sign of God's merciful grace made room for me and my sisters and brothers united by our ancestors to become whole again. Our fragmented selves were given sight to see one another, and the continued ceremony of the African traditional community was embodied and for me, this brought forth an everlasting breath of knowing thy self.[23]

---

23 Antoinette Kemp, personal correspondence, November 2010.

The ceremony held at Elmina, the exact site of the landing in 1471 of the first Europeans on the West Coast of Africa, on 1 August 2007, is a telling example of constructive postcolonializing African practical theology. In all these ways the reality of a traumatic past was faced and new possibilities for a tragic people forged. This African liturgy demonstrated that with courage and theological creativity, redemptive postcolonializing liturgies can be created for even as devastating an occurrence as the Transatlantic slave trade that can have a lasting impact for good on the lives of persons globally.

4

Transcending Colonial Religion: Brother Ishmael Tetteh and the Etherean Mission

Born in Ghana, then the British colony named the Gold Coast, on 19 September 1953 Ishmael Nyarku Oblitey Tetteh appeared destined for the mystical life from birth. His father, Humphrey Commey Tetteh, was himself gifted in praying especially for the healing of the sick. His mother's name is Florence Dei Djanie. Ishmael is the twelfth born of his father and the seventh of his mother. The young Ishmael observed his father's practices of prayer and laying hands on people for healing and early in life participated in prayer and healing activities with him. At age five Ishmael prayed for and healed one of his cousins.[1]

Through his teenage years Brother Ishmael continued in an earnest search for God, fuelled particularly by the deaths of two dear ones of his – his father, when Ishmael was 14 years old, and his school teacher, Mrs Chinery. These deaths raised questions concerning the meaning of life and death in young Ishmael. Why had such noble, illustrious, kind, caring and thoughtful people died? What was this thing called life? Baptized in the Methodist Church, Ishmael became a Jehovah's Witness but soon disagreed with their teachings and followed the faith his father had adopted – the Apostolic faith. Following his father's death, Ishmael flirted with the Baptist tradition before returning to his Methodist roots.

---

[1] Ishmael N. O. Tetteh, *The Inspired African Mystical Gospel*, Accra: Etherean Mission Publishing, 2001, p. 11.

So intense was his search for God that young Ishmael did not hesitate to walk five miles from school to the beach every Friday evening to pray. He would walk eight miles back home when he was done praying. The Bible was a close companion which he read constantly, and also engaged in the random opening of it for guidance which he believed he received from God at specific times especially when he needed some assurance in times of difficulty.

Tetteh relates having a deeply mystical experience at age 19, which was difficult to describe. His encounter seems similar to occurrences which many mystics in different settings have also written about. While praying at the beach, 'a presence appeared to me. I was suddenly in a place of beauty and life; it seemed to be a city where everything [was] alive and all beings communicate[d] without words. I could feel and know that I was in a divine field of beauty and power. To describe this wonderful experience is to profane it.'[2] Over the weeks following this experience, Tetteh describes 'callings' and 'knowings' which in significant ways were a challenge to his own faith, what he had been taught and his sense of what was right. These experiences, though, were the beginnings and markers of a path which led into the core objectives of the mission and gathering of mystics that formed around him.

In the first of these he describes being once again in the 'divine energy field of presence' and being instructed to 'perform blessings of all the rivers in the land (of Ghana)'.[3] Tetteh's recounting of his reaction points both to the dilemma he found himself in at this instruction and to the recovery of African traditional religious beliefs embedded within it.

> I considered this demand as fetish, knowing it to be the thing that the [African] traditional priests do. I have been brought up to consider everything African as evil. To do this requirement was very evil to me. I then wondered if I have accidentally tripped into the trap of the so-called devil. A divine knowing within me tells me I have to do it. To settle the matter, I had

---

2 Tetteh, *The Inspired African Mystical Gospel*, pp. 12–13.
3 Tetteh, *The Inspired African Mystical Gospel*, p. 13.

to, as usual consult the Bible, which I did. I prayed and opened the Bible three times. I read passages in the Bible that informed me that 'God is no respecter of persons and that in every land, whoever does his will is accepted of Him' (Acts 10.34). Another reading told me that 'there is nothing unclean of itself and that whoever considers anything to be unclean, to him it is unclean.' (Romans 14.14) ... A third reading told me that 'unto the pure all things are pure but that it is the defiled mind that considers things as unclean'.[4]

Brother Ishmael went ahead and performed the rites as he was instructed, consecrating the rivers of the land. At every site and rite of consecration he reports that 'the spirit presence of God manifested to me and a teaching on the oneness of life and of mankind, irrespective of race, creed or culture incarnated in me'.[5] Tetteh's retelling of what he describes as his 'initiation' bears the very hallmarks of mysticism:

> as I prayed at my altar ... I was drawn into a great darkness. A darkness so fearsome, dense, awesome yet alive with energy. A darkness that speaks of all things. A part of me was afraid because it had been taught that darkness is evil. It seemed to be an eternity of fight between my fear and the darkness. At last, the knowing from my experience with the consecration of the waters sparked a knowing in me that all things must be God.[6]

An intriguing aspect of Tetteh's experience of the divine presence was that the resplendent indescribable beauty of the presence which he encountered was 'not masculine, not feminine but more feminine'.[7] Tetteh is baffled, perplexed but instructed by the 'beauty that I instantly called my Mother, my woman, my angel,

---

4 Tetteh, *The Inspired African Mystical Gospel*, pp. 13–14.
5 Tetteh, *The Inspired African Mystical Gospel*, p. 14.
6 Tetteh, *The Inspired African Mystical Gospel*, p. 14.
7 Tetteh, *The Inspired African Mystical Gospel*, p. 15.

spirit of my heart, the heart of my soul, my queen of all perfection'.[8] He writes,

> The idea of God being a woman was in itself blasphemous; how could I speak of my Madonna as I called the HOLY PRESENCE – the feminine manifestation of God to me? From that moment I knew all things that I needed to know. I knew the true omnipresence of God; the holiness of God within African religion and the acceptability of all religions to the one omnific loving God; the absolute goodness of God without an opposite called a devil. I realized that in teaching, such knowledge would be considered blasphemous. My spirit was however certain of my unique mission and I was determined to follow through.[9]

This mystic revelation was contrary to much of what he had been taught. His experience stretched him out and awakened in him a knowing that he has sought to be faithful to since 1973, when it all began to unfold.

Beginning in the early 1970s, Ishmael Tetteh became a spiritual magnet for an expanding group of people drawn to the message of liberty and transcendence that he taught and practised. The Etherean Mission which emerged was energized by a mystical spirituality that was both instructive and practical. It transcended the denominationalism, religious elitism, clericalism and separatism for which missionary Christianity as well as orthodox Islam had become well known. Above all perhaps, was its revaluing and re-appropriating of the religious heritage of Africa which had been so denigrated and demonized by the religions of West and East that have been imported into the country. The Etherean Mission was officially inaugurated in 1975.[10] The three main objectives of the Etherean Mission are:

---

8 Tetteh, *The Inspired African Mystical Gospel*, p. 15.
9 Tetteh, *The Inspired African Mystical Gospel*, p. 15.
10 Tetteh, *The Inspired African Mystical Gospel*, p. 19. The Etherean Mission now exists also in the United Kingdom and Malawi. In the USA, Brother Tetteh's work has been formalized into an organization known as 'Conscious Humanity Inc.' based in Los Angeles, California – see www.conscioushumanity.org.

- To bring spiritual enlightenment to mankind.
- To create a platform for religious oneness.
- To restore the Mystical traditions of Africa.[11]

Brother Ishmael Tetteh recognizes the ancestors as his source of knowledge and teaching.[12] He is convinced that all religious traditions have something valid to contribute to the spiritual well-being of humanity. These beliefs have resulted in much persecution and name calling. He writes:

> I have been persecuted by brainwashed Africans for teaching my belief in the divinity and sanctity of African religions and cultures. Africans have been so much conditioned to the belief that everything African is evil. The result is that Africans look down on their rich cultural and spiritual heritage. The custodians of the African knowledge system are unwilling to teach it to those who may profane it and thus die with their rich spiritual knowledge . . . I have been persecuted and still being persecuted for teaching the oneness of God, of man, and of religion. Christians consider me a non-Christian for my belief in other religions and my references from other religious materials and the Moslems in my country cannot fit me into the Islamic tradition. Traditionalists would want me to take a full stand for them and only them. But I am here to dissolve factionalism and remove barriers and not add to the already saturated life full of barriers.[13]

In spite of several attempts by people to confer other honorific titles upon him, Ishmael Tetteh prefers to be called 'a brother', because he says:

---

11 Ishmael N. O. Tetteh, *Etherean Mission Handbook*, Accra: Asante & Hittscher Press, n. d., p. 14.

12 Tetteh acknowledges African as well as Hindu, Islamic and Western ancestors as his mentors and teachers. For such categorical acknowledgement see *The Inspired African Mystical Gospel*, pp. 9, 17.

13 Tetteh, *The Inspired African Mystical Gospel*, p. 19.

I believe in the brotherhood of man based on what we truly are as spiritual beings and the sons and daughters of God. I am looking for a world in which there will be no ranks and titles that divide the people. Titles will be right when they complement the glory of God in another person. I am a spiritual nomad; everywhere I go is home and everyone I meet is my brother and sister.[14]

My approach in this chapter, and in what follows, is to give privilege and pride of place to Brother Tetteh himself. I have had several conversations with him and have sought to clarify what I have understood in order to truly represent his life and teaching instead of imposing my personal or disciplinary interpretive lens that would not do him justice. I have quoted extensively from his voluminous writings – already amounting to 25 books – in line with this approach. In order for an appreciation of Tetteh's postcolonializing efforts, this seemed to me the most effective way forward. I present the material under the headings of the three objectives claimed by the Etherean Mission.

Spiritual enlightenment for all humanity

In a book titled *The Fountain of Life: A Course in Metaphysics*, first published in 1975, Ishmael Tetteh outlines the essential inner core of the teachings that undergird his life and ministry.[15] Metaphysics is understood as 'the spiritual understanding of the scriptures'.[16] It is not a religion in itself but rather the 'science of religion',[17] 'a study of the spirituality of religion'.[18] Tetteh is keen to promote an understanding of religion and the scriptures through study and the application in practice of principles of life. To understand scriptures

---

14 Tetteh, *The Inspired African Mystical Gospel*, p. 22.
15 Ishmael Tetteh, *The Fountain of Life: A Course in Metaphysics*, Accra, Ghana: The Etherean Mission, 1999.
16 Tetteh, *Fountain of Life*, p. 13.
17 Tetteh, *Fountain of Life*, p. 13.
18 Tetteh, *Fountain of Life*, p. 16.

effectively, he argues, they must be studied in the spirit of the author. To do so readers must be prepared to be transported in consciousness 'to the time, culture and the circumstance within which the teaching was shared'.[19] Thus, he clearly indicates the importance of studying texts in their context. He is also concerned that practitioners be not frozen in time in their spiritual practice, but rather that while spiritual principles may not change, they must be translated to be applicable to the current circumstance. 'The religion that does not evolve scientifically eventually dies.'[20]

Tetteh's attitude to the scriptures of various religious traditions, far from being literalistic or dogmatic, is respectful yet critical, inquiring and open. He declares, 'religion becomes a cult when it limits your thinking to a set of established norms. Religion must on the reverse, be the opening of one's consciousness to explore and enjoy the infinite.' He goes on to argue that 'Holy books such as the Bible, Qur'an and Bhagavad Gita must be used as tools that open the consciousness of men. These books would become tools of bondage when they are used as the ceiling to religious and life study.'[21] Tetteh, accordingly, is not shy of raising questions and critiquing biblical texts, the main Scriptures he refers to in his books. Though not a scholar of biblical languages, and without claims to being a scholarly text, Tetteh's book contains a section of 'Bible Contradictions'[22] in which several obvious discrepancies and inconsistencies in word and allusion are stated. Tetteh concludes that 'when it comes to scriptural matters, the Bible and any other religious book for that matter cannot be said to be the only authority'.[23] 'The Bible is neither the earliest nor the final authority on God and the Truth of life. The Bible is not a recording of direct instructions and messages from God.'[24] In fact, in line with a deep and high regard for the spiritual essence within human beings, about which we shall have more to say, Ishmael Tetteh

---

19 Tetteh, *Fountain of Life*, p. 13.
20 Tetteh, *Fountain of Life*, p. 13.
21 Tetteh, *Fountain of Life*, p. 14.
22 Tetteh, *Fountain of Life*, pp. 178–83.
23 Tetteh, *Fountain of Life*, p. 176.
24 Tetteh, *Fountain of Life*, p. 177.

teaches that 'the real Bible is within man. The truth is within you and you have to draw your attention within and find out the inner meaning of what you read.'[25] For Tetteh, the Bible, though not a direct word from God, 'was written from inspiration by people who could commune with Omniscience and tap relevant information'.[26] As such 'enlightened souls can, through meditation and ardent search for the truth, be exposed to the inner meanings of these stories'.[27] His conclusion is that the Scriptures (of the various religious traditions) 'should therefore be read with a discerning mind so that one can derive the deeper meanings of the lessons they purport to teach and apply them in our lives'.[28]

The Fountain of Life is a collection of fifteen lessons providing knowledge and understanding of mystical subjects, which constitute the foundation of all the teachings of the Etherean Mission. It is directed and dedicated to 'all students of the mystical path' with special reference and acknowledgement to all Ethereans worldwide. Brother Ishmael Tetteh asserts that the topics covered in the book are discussed from time to time as the main syllabus of the Mission and this process of discussion helps in the growth of members of the Mission. Each chapter (lesson) ends with a summary ('what you have learnt so far'), practical application of the topic, affirmations and concludes with a set of questions for 'self-processing'. The emphasis clearly is upon practical mysticism in both tone and the exercises offered. The reader is invited to engage in the applications, write and reflect on lessons learned and to actually declare the affirmations and by this means derive some benefit from the spiritual technologies on offer.

On God: the absolute beyond and within all

The first full lesson is appropriately contained in a chapter on 'God'. Tetteh argues that God is the Intelligent, All-pervading,

---

25 Tetteh, *Fountain of Life*, p. 177.
26 Tetteh, *Fountain of Life*, p. 183.
27 Tetteh, *Fountain of Life*, p. 183.
28 Tetteh, *Fountain of Life*, p. 184.

All-prevailing Power and Presence behind all that exists. 'God is the governing principle, energy and law operating in, through and as all things.'[29] God is as such also the 'awesome energy' behind every human being and all of humanity. God, it is, that maintains the 'universe including you in perfect order'.[30]

If by personal we mean a physical entity with attributes such as humans have, then that for Tetteh is not what God is like. 'God is not merely a person as we humans think of "persons". God is the Intelligent Energy that constitutes all of life and that everyone is an expression of. God cannot be Omnipresent without being present in everyone. Since God is Omnipotent and Omniscient His/Her greatness permeates all life.'[31]

Tetteh seriously doubts and rejects seven notions of God which he finds not only unappealing but destructive. These are: (1) The *Sectarian God*, who is simply the 'God' of a sect. 'He may be a Christian "God" or Hindu "God" or Moslem "God" etc. He loves only the people of his sect and mercilessly punishes people of all other sects eternally.'[32] (2) The *Judgmental God*, 'a white bearded old man who sits far [away] in the skies and is looking upon the earth with eagle eyes to see who does or does not do his will. His anger rises and falls like human beings but he is possibly more cruel than most humans. For example, he has created a place called hell where all those who do not do his will, will be roasted eternally after their death.'[33] (3) The *Semi-Powerful God*, who in spite of being known as 'good' has created another powerful being like himself called 'the devil' to challenge himself and has decreed that any human who may succumb to this creature's luring will burn eternally in fire with him at an unknown date when presumably this creature will finally be overcome. (4) The *Gender God* – believed to be a male so is best approached solely by males. To this 'God' females are inferior and must not stand

---

29 Tetteh, *Fountain of Life*, p. 40.
30 Tetteh, *Fountain of Life*, p. 40.
31 Ishmael Tetteh, *The Mission of Jesus Revealed*, Accra: Etherean Mission Publishing, 2011, p. 15.
32 Tetteh, *Fountain of Life*, p. 34.
33 Tetteh, *Fountain of Life*, p. 34.

in the most holy places of his shrines else they incur his anger. This 'God' particularly hates women when they are in their menstrual period. 'He is very strong in our homes where he makes every male the ruler.' (5) The *Remote Control God* – this 'God' is far away from this unclean earth and remotely controls all things here from his far away heavenly abode. (6) The *Racial God* – who accepts only people of specific races and cultures while rejecting the rest. In an obvious reference to the activities of some missionaries, Tetteh illustrates, '[F]or you to be accepted by him you have to relinquish your name, creed and culture and follow the culture of this "God's" preferred race.'[34] (7) The *Blood Thirsty God* – requires the blood of animals to appease his wrath and to coerce him to forgive wrongs. This God has called for the blood of his only begotten son for there to be total remission of sins.

Rejecting each of these 'gods', Tetteh affirms the Omnipotent, Omnipresent, Omniscient God:

> This 'God' is the very energy of life, present in all things as the substance of all things. He is a Father–Mother God, balanced as the polarity of sexes. He-She embodies the entire universe as its substance, energy, law and cohesive love. All things dwell and have their existence in Him-Her. He-She is the only power, wisdom and presence there is. This is my God.[35]

One intriguing aspect of Tetteh's theology, to which we shall return in a later section, is the insistence upon both genders when referring to the divine. God is Father–Mother. Ishmael Tetteh by birth and parentage belongs to the Gã ethnic group of Accra in Ghana. The Gã name for God is *Ataa Naa Nyɔŋmɔ* which literally translates as 'Great-Father Great-Mother God'. Unlike the English language the Gã is non-sexist in its third-person pronoun and in reference to God employs bisexual titles. Tetteh's language for God is reminiscent of this without a descent into racial or tribal exclusivism. Throughout his writing and in his public teaching and prayers, Tetteh unfailingly refers to God as 'Mother-Father God'.

---

34 Tetteh, *Fountain of Life*, p. 35.
35 Tetteh, *Fountain of Life*, p. 36.

On the Christ: the divinity of humanity

Tetteh's views on the central plank of Christian orthodoxy would be considered unconventional even heretical. He recognizes this and affirms himself 'non-denominational'. He asserts, 'I am simply a practical mystical Christian, following the teachings of Jesus and ignoring "popular Christianity".'[36] Tetteh affirms a Trinitarian belief. To illustrate this and the particular nuances he brings to this doctrine it is necessary to quote him extensively here:

> God is one but in attribute he is two expressed as **Father and Mother**; wisdom and intelligence, motion and stability; positive and negative; yet in essence he is three. The third member is that force that holds the two poles of North and South together. This force is the only begotten of Father-Mother God and is responsible for the total expression of the attributes of Father-Mother God, in the same way as the electrical force of the magnet is responsible for the expression of the attributes of its north and south poles. This expression is the process of creation and the drama of life. Almighty God cannot exist without him, so He was in the beginning with God and all things were made by Him and without Him was not anything made that was made . . . (St John 1:1–4). This force is called Christ, the only begotten of Almighty God, the God of Force and God Omniscient, God of thought and Christ is God, the God of love – Divine Love.[37]

Christ the Universal Love is pervasive throughout the cosmos. Tetteh explains that the word 'Christ' means 'the anointed one' and is an official title which means 'Master of Divine Love'. Thus 'when we say Jesus the Christ we refer to the man and to his office just as we do when we say Dora the nurse or Ishmael the minister or Mustapha the doctor'.[38] Jesus then attains the title 'the Christ' through his obedience and discipline. For Tetteh, Divine Christ or

---

36 Tetteh, *Fountain of Life*, p. 185.
37 Tetteh, *Fountain of Life*, p. 186.
38 Tetteh, *Fountain of Life*, p. 191.

Divine Love has been manifest in other Masters such as Krishna, Buddha, Muhammad and others as well. Tetteh declares,

> The Christ consciousness is the universal consciousness of Love and has incarnated in many men (sic) of various ages and generations to remind men (sic) of their real relationship with God.[39]

Jesus did manifest the Christ, but he made it clear that all the 'works' he had done could be done by those who believed (John 14.12), demonstrating that the 'miracles are the fruits of the Christ [and] were thus displayed to prove the possibilities of man [sic] when he allows the Christ to manifest in him through discipline'.[40] Jesus lived to demonstrate human possibilities and capabilities. What Jesus did can also be done by those who follow him. By declaring that 'the kingdom of God is within you' (Luke 17.21, NIV mg), that 'you are the light of the world' (Matt. 5.14), 'you are the salt of the earth' (Matt. 5.13), and that 'you are gods' (John 10.34), Tetteh is emphatic that Jesus teaches that humanity in its spiritual state is divine.[41] Tetteh sums up the mission of Jesus as having three objectives: (a) to teach the divinity of humanity, and its practice that gives us absolute empowerment; (b) to unite humanity as one family of God by dissolving all religious and political barriers and enforce the spiritual practice of having a single vision; (c) to teach respect for one's self and one's culture.[42]

On humanity: divinely earthy

In a chapter titled 'Man', Ishmael Tetteh engages his theological anthropology more fully. Tetteh is very definitely non-sexist, so it is clear that this usage, which is present in all his works, reflects the difficulties of the English language rather than any lack of sensitivity on his part. This is also the case with his usage of the

---

39 Tetteh, *Fountain of Life*, p. 194.
40 Tetteh, *Fountain of Life*, p. 189.
41 Tetteh, *Mission of Jesus*, pp. 29–46.
42 Tetteh, *Mission of Jesus*, pp. 26–7.

Authorized Version (the King James translation) of the Bible in all – including very recent – publications of his. It is of significance that he employs colonial tools in his postcolonial debunking and reframing of the teaching he received as a child, through school and church. Quintessentially a postcolonializer, Tetteh employs the archaic language and the trappings of colonialism in order to subvert and disrupt the hegemonic power of that very language and its colonial religious structures.

Tetteh's anthropology is in many ways theological, spiritual and mystical. Human beings are spiritual beings endowed with all the capabilities of spirit. A human is a blending of divine qualities in mind and emotion, with a body. Humans are full of vast innate potential. For Tetteh the essential, indeed the *real*, human being is spirit. 'It is therefore necessary to give more attention to the things that concern real man and not his outer coat of material body.'[43] However this is not Greco-Roman dualism with a denigration of the body and elevation of the spirit. Tetteh and his circle have formulated a series of technologies and exercises, called Etherean Mission Application Technology (EMAT), 'for social, emotional, psychological, financial and physical well being'.[44] 'Man', asserts Tetteh, 'is the greatest revelation of God and his mind is the greatest tool in him.'[45] Making reference to the Bhagavad Gita Tetteh asserts that 'Real man is eternal'. 'For the soul there is never birth nor death, nor once having been does he ever cease to be. He is unborn, eternal, everlasting, undying and primeval. He is not slain when the body is slain.'[46]

In characterizations which echo the traditional beliefs of the Gã people of Ghana, the difference between the human and the animal lies in the degree of intelligence. While animals have sense, humans are very much more intelligent as is evidenced in the scientific, economic and social inventions that humanity has achieved. Humans are here on this earth to experience the fullness of who they each are as beloved children of God. Within human persons is an

---

43 Tetteh, *Mission of Jesus*, p. 51.
44 Tetteh, *Etherean Mission Handbook*, p. 53.
45 Tetteh, *Etherean Mission Handbook*, p. 79.
46 Tetteh, *Fountain of Life*, p. 51.

'impulsive drive' to discover and know themselves. When this drive is not truly satisfied, humans are filled with sorrow. Our physical bodies are needed in order for us to gain experience in life on earth. For human beings to be truly happy and fulfilled we must study and gain spiritual knowledge. 'Teaching people merely to survive is not pure and total education; to eat, mate, sleep and enjoy life is beastly; a pure and total education must give birth to the unfoldment [sic] of one's inner capabilities and possibilities.'[47]

Tetteh holds to a very high anthropology. Every human person is an expression of the divine Creator. The created is of the same substance as the Creator. As such each human is a 'unit of cosmic consciousness'. He writes, 'you are a wave on the mighty ocean. You are not the ocean yet you are neither separate nor apart from it.'[48] To explain this further, Tetteh calls upon his readers to imagine the space where they are to be the entire universe. Only Omnipresent God fills the space. Should God decide then to create, the only material God has to create with would be God's self. God can only use God self to create since there is no other presence. 'Everything created was created by God and placed in the substance of God.'[49] He cites Acts 17.28, 'In him we live, and move, and have our being' and from the Bhagavad Gita, 'I am the original seed of all existence', in support of his notion that God is manifest in every unit of life.

The true inner core and essence of humanity is spirit. 'Man', writes Tetteh, 'is essentially a spirit being'.[50] Other aspects of human nature are understood as clothes that are put on for various conditions and purposes. Humanity first puts on mental clothing like we would underwear. Next, emotional clothes like one would put on a dress or shirt. Finally, the physical body is put on like a coat. All three sets of clothing or 'bodies' are interlinked with the mental and emotional ones being most closely connected. One becomes a living

---

47 Tetteh, *Fountain of Life*, p. 52.
48 Tetteh, *Fountain of Life*, p. 69.
49 Tetteh, *Fountain of Life*, p. 69.
50 Ishmael N. O. Tetteh, *Soul Processing: The Path to Freedom. A Revolutionary Spiritual Mind Science for Total Well Being*, Accra: The Etherean Mission, 1997, p. 41.

soul when all of these clothes have been worn. This is how Brother Tetteh describes it:

> When the spirit, the pure beingness of man, takes on any or all of these vehicles, it then becomes a soul or psyche. A soul is, therefore, the spirit identified with mind and matter. In body form the spirit is able to express all of its attributes at any given time.[51]

In Brother Tetteh's reckoning by far the most significant gift to and of humanity is the mind. Mind is energy imbued with creative and discriminative reasoning. It is through the mind and its senses that we receive and transmit information. In keeping with his high anthropology, human beings are individualized spirit beings that are pure, holy and glorious from the start. This spirit being essentially embraces Christ-like virtues and qualities and is averse to anything short of these. Goodness, happiness, pleasure, and joy are understood by individualized mind as the goals of life. Opposite to these and directed against them is pain. 'Pain, whether real or threatened, is understood as the force opposing the spirit's will to be.'[52]

In terms of gender identity and role, Tetteh's teaching suggests that human beings mirror and express the bisexual divine nature. He writes: 'Each individual is the embodiment of both male and female aspects of God. But physically you are wearing a male or female garment to help you accomplish a specific purpose – to provide a service.'[53]

On the devil: the power of an illusion

A truly remarkable aspect of Ishmael Tetteh's teaching is the belief in the non-existence of the devil as an entity or power opposed to God's existence and plan. For Ethereans, 'the only evil on earth is destructive thinking'.[54] Tetteh argues thus, 'Man is pure, but when

---

51 Tetteh, *Soul Processing*, p. 41.
52 Tetteh, *Soul Processing*, p. 45.
53 Tetteh, *The Inspired African Mystical Gospel*, p. 151.
54 Tetteh, *Fountain of Life*, p. 83.

infested with the forces that lead to destruction and in opposition to the evolutionary process, evil is born.'[55] In the *Etherean Mission Handbook*, under a section on the 'Fundamental teaching', we find the following extract concerning the 'devil':

> No earthly parent would lock up their children in a room with a poisonous snake to haunt them. And if we are this loving, we must credit God with much more love. The bible says in Matthew 7:11, *'If ye then, being evil, know how to give good gifts unto your children, how much more shall your Father which is in heaven give good things to them that ask him?'* A loving God will not allow such an entity to sabotage his excellent creation. Such would mean that God has defeated himself. It is irrational to think that God would create another power like himself to sabotage him.[56]

For Tetteh, to acknowledge another power besides God is to worship another god besides God which is idolatry. Moreover, to label any part of the universe as evil is to label a part of God as evil which is also mental idolatry.[57] In a radical monism, Tetteh admonishes his hearers to accept God as all that there is so that our conciousness becomes full of God. Such a God-filled consciousness is his understanding of salvation.

Evil spirits do not exist as entities. Rather these (such as Lucifer, Beelzebub, Satan etc.) are 'congregated thought forces of hate, envy, jealousy, anger, apathy, etc'.[58] Tetteh is convinced that 'as he thinketh in his heart, so is he' (Prov. 23.7, AV). 'The collected power of all misguided thought forces of all beings, incarnate and discarnate form the big mental energy field of Lucifer, Asmodey and Beelzebub.'[59] Thus evil is real and has effect, not because it is caused by some created personified god-like power, but rather through misguided, destructive thinking by individuals which

---

55 Tetteh, *Fountain of Life*, p. 83.
56 Tetteh, *Etherean Mission Handbook*, p. 85.
57 Tetteh, *Fountain of Life*, p. 84.
58 Tetteh, *Fountain of Life*, p. 85.
59 Tetteh, *Fountain of Life*, p. 85.

when aggregated by groups of people can be devastating in its effects. Tetteh is clear and emphatic on this:

> The devil as an entity created by God does not exist. However, if you describe a thing for a long time, even though the thing does not exist in reality, it is created for you as your personal experience. Know that creative energy follows your belief system made up of your thoughts, feelings and words. We know of people who tell a particular piece of lie for a long time until it becomes real in their consciousness and outer experience. There certainly is a devil created by the thoughts of those that believe in it and have described it and that mental devil does claw its victims who believe in its existence.[60]

On desire: a double-edged sword

There are two aspects of the human being that Ishmael Tetteh very highly values. These are the mind and the emotions. To him mind is the arbiter of all that is, and can reach to the most sublime heaven as well as descend to the lowest abyss. Mind, for him, has four sections which he terms (a) the conscious mind, (b) the subconscious mind, (c) the unconscious mind, and (d) the superconscious mind. He goes on to divide the conscious mind into the *suggestible* and the *reasoning* mind.

Tracing the path of any thought that occurs to us, Tetteh presents an explanation of the functions of each of these aspects of mind. When a thought enters our minds it first registers in the suggestible part of the conscious mind. The idea or suggestion is then transferred to the reasoning mind. It is at this section that the idea is analysed for action. If it is not acceptable it is dropped. If it is acceptable, it registers and the body is instructed to act on it. If the idea is acceptable but action is delayed it is transferred to the subconscious mind for storage until an opportune time for action. The subconscious mind is thus the storehouse or reservoir

---

60 Tetteh, *Fountain of Life*, p. 136.

for all thoughts, ideas and suggestions that the mind accepts but on which action is delayed. The subconscious mind then automatically generates all stored mental impressions. An understanding of this, Tetteh claims, can help us to shape and reshape our destiny by feeding the subconscious with the needed desires. Tetteh teaches that 'the subconscious mind works best in our sleep state and sometimes gives us useful information but in crazy jigsaw puzzles which we call dreams'.[61] 'This sub-conscious mind appears to be dormant or inactive, but in the mechanism of the mind it is a very active and powerful force because it keeps on releasing these stored ideas from time to time.'[62]

While the subconscious mind stores what the mind accepts but cannot act upon immediately, the unconscious mind files all the information that cannot be presently handled by an individual. The vast majority of such material has to do with pain, since pain is that which we most shy away from, hide from or are unable to handle. The unconscious mind stores all such information until the individual is ready to handle it. The unconscious mind files this information in pictorial form and includes all sense perceptions that occur at the time of the incident whose information it is keeping. Information in the unconscious mind remains hidden until it is re-stimulated by encounters which evoke any of the sensory picture elements stored in connection with the occurrences, usually the pain-filled incidents. When this happens, the information surfaces to the subconscious mind where one is driven to re-experience the pain. Painful pictures from the past constantly interfere with present positive desires. In order to have a dynamic and creative mind it is necessary to cleanse the unconscious mind of all its past pains.[63] The superconscious mind is conceived of as the 'spiritual mind and seat of God' in the human person.[64]

---

61 Tetteh, *Fountain of Life*, p. 93.
62 Tetteh, *Fountain of Life*, pp. 93–4.
63 A process for this cleansing has been formulated by the Etherean Mission and is called 'Soul Processing'. We shall be discussing the process more fully as an example of the Mission's forms of spiritual care.
64 Tetteh, *Fountain of Life*, p. 95.

Closely associated with mind is desire. Desire arises mostly from the stored information made up of emotions in the subconscious mind. Nevertheless desire, he argues, is a creative instrument given to humanity which can create both good and ill. Not only is desire natural it is also very useful for survival in this world. Desire is a key ingredient for successful living for it carries a motive power for implementation. Without it we court failure regardless of how talented or intelligent we may be. Desire draws in energy to focus one's attention on what is already in existence universally.

For Tetteh, 'all desires are various forms of God's manifestations'.[65] In order to create the good we wish for, he suggests, desire has to be intense, sustained and backed by action. For desire to be perfect and produce good, it must have spiritual insight and its fulfilment must satisfy a necessity that is beneficial to the universe.

On the purpose of humanity: karma, reincarnation and liberation

Rejecting a 'mundane theory' which would consider the existence of humanity as a chance event subject only to science which ends in death; and a 'theological' theory in which a powerful deity creates human beings to please his whims, and in which a human being's obedience to the deity's commands ensures an eternity of bliss while disobedience results in 'everlasting roasting in hell', Brother Ishmael Tetteh expounds a 'metaphysical theory' in which humanity is an expression of God. Human beings are to unfold and express their divine capabilities through several incarnations until perfection is attained. Maintenance on the path of full expression is ascertained by the feedback system known as the law of karma which prompts humans on to perfection.

In this teaching, life is a continuous and gradual process of the unfolding of God. Birth is not the beginning of a soul's life and physical death is not the end. The soul is eternal, existing in an un-manifest state until birth. Souls travel from the first moments

---

65 Tetteh, *Fountain of Life*, p. 97.

of manifestation of earth life through a series of incarnations till they attain perfect knowledge. This knowledge reveals the limitless potential of God expressing in and as the soul. The whole goal and purpose of life is maturity and the way to its attainment life experience. The 'feedback system' known as the law of *karma* (explained by reference to the word's Sanskrit origins, 'cause and effect') is designed to help each soul unfold, grow and express its limitless potential.[66] This law, says Tetteh, 'projects the errors as well as the achievements before the individualized soul either for their correction or to spur him on to the unfoldment [sic] of the greater glories or more dynamic potential'.[67] Any deficit in maturity calls for some experience, joyous or painful, to help rectify or supply what is needed. If one is unable to accomplish this unfolding prior to one's death, the deity assists one to reincarnate into conditions that will help in the onward journey towards maturity. People may as such go through some challenges in life not because of a previous emotional or mental cause but for the purpose of growth or maturity. The Karmic law then, for Tetteh, is a law of our own being for the realization of our own potentialities not an operative energy to punish or reward but rather to correct and redirect.

To be liberated is then a function of our ability to learn the correcting and redirecting lessons of life. Brother Tetteh writes, 'to liberate oneself therefore, one must be alert to assimilate quickly the lessons from the seemingly good rewards as well as the evil appearances. For, every appearance of good as well as evil, are simply teachers to lead us to higher grounds, only when their lessons have been learnt.'[68] Life experience and the Karmic law are about choices and counter-choices. Life's quest is for wise choices. Many people do not exercise their right and ability to make conscious choices. They unconsciously simply choose to be affected by whatever happens around them. It is crucial that we be conscious of our choices and their effects.

---

66 Tetteh, *Fountain of Life*, p. 103.
67 Tetteh, *Fountain of Life*, p. 103.
68 Tetteh, *Fountain of Life*, p. 113.

In sum, for Tetteh, there is a natural law operative in the universe which gives each human being feedback concerning their thoughts and actions in past and present lives. This is not about punishments or rewards but rather feedback on the results of our actions for reappraisal and correction. Nature by this law directs our endeavours towards the sole goal of life – perfection. These natural promptings confront us in the form of repeated experiences of the same or similar incidents until we learn from their lessons.

Through a spiritual discipline (called in the Etherean Mission a spiritual 'technology') known as Soul Processing, which we discuss later, and especially a procedure called 'Karma Transmutation', Tetteh offers a way of maximizing and speeding up the karmic experience of repeated incarnations. Essentially the technique is based on understanding that 'present experience contains within it seeds of knowing, truth revealing and freedom'.[69] With this understanding every current experience is accepted as an opportunity for the revelation of divine virtues that will be a blessing to life. With each experience we ask ourselves 'What learning is there in this experience for me or for my environment?' Choosing to learn the lesson implicit in the experience then renders the need for its repetition in another lifetime unnecessary. Tetteh sums it up in this way:

> What you are today is the sum total of all your thoughts, feelings and actions of yesterday. The technique is to think right, feel right and act right for a right future. You are in control of your future.[70]

By seeing our thoughts, feelings and actions as causes we can consciously generate a different outcome for ourselves and our environment, through wise and positive choices of thought, feeling and action.

---

69 Tetteh, *Fountain of Life*, p. 117.
70 Tetteh, *Fountain of Life*, p. 119.

On communion with the divine: prayer, meditation and fasting

In Etherean Mission, prayer is defined as 'the scientific method of harnessing the Emotional, Mental and Physical faculties of our being into recognition and experience of the absoluteness of God.'[71]

Brother Tetteh understands the universe as the 'body of God'. God is love and as such the universe is held together by the cohesive force of love. Everything we need is already in existence. Prayer is one of the powerful tools which bring us to the point of opening ourselves for that which already is, to flow in and through us. Prayer therefore does not change God. Instead it has the potential to change the one praying. Tetteh declares, 'we cannot use our prayers to influence God or make him change his mind about anything or anybody. We would be underrating him if we think we could ... We cannot say that our prayers influence God else God would be subservient to prayer. What prayer does is to make us see and claim our heritage as God's children.'[72]

Prayer then is more than a momentary action. Indeed our 'very life-styles should be a form of prayer, for prayer is a way of life'.[73] Fulfilment of prayer may also be expedited when we are tuned to the consciousness of a known spiritual leader or authority. Quoting the Gospels, Tetteh argues that Jesus said, 'if ye love me, keep my commandments'. In order that prayer be acceptable, the disciple should be devoted to the Master and make alive the Master's teachings in his or her life. Such a disciple can then ask for anything in the Master's consciousness or name and it would be given them. Further, Jesus said (John 15.7, AV) 'if ye abide in me, and my words abide in you, ye shall ask what ye will, and it shall be done unto you'. As such the effort to make our lives pure and truthful is also prayer, since it draws us to the divine goodness and love. 'To abide in Jesus is to abide in his fearless, truthful

---

71 Tetteh, *Fountain of Life*, p. 124.
72 Tetteh, *Fountain of Life*, p. 124.
73 Tetteh, *Fountain of Life*, p. 127.

and Godchild consciousness. You must, like Jesus, abide in the awareness that you are a divine child of a divine Father-Mother God... When you live in such a consciousness you walk divinely tall and filled with a perfect spiritual confidence in which you say, "be" and it is.'[74]

The crux of the matter of prayer for Tetteh is awakening to truth. 'The highest form of prayer does not consist in the actual act of praying but in awakening to the truth, the Christ of our being. When this state is reached diseases disappear, sins are destroyed and death becomes non-existent.'[75] The crucial thing then is being awakened to the truth, for when we awaken to truth faith follows automatically – a faith that is not blind but based on knowing. Fear, Tetteh explains, is the opposite of faith. For the one who awakens to God, and knows who God is, there is no fear that God will not answer prayer. Fear blocks the flow by turning off our 'receiving station' thus preventing us from receiving what God is already doing. Fear is the negation of prayer. Applying a principle based on Proverbs 23.7 (AV), 'as he thinketh in his heart so is he', Brother Tetteh argues that fear attracts us to that which we fear. Instead, 'whatever things you desire, when you pray believe that you have received them and you shall have them' (Matt. 21.22), consequently, 'to believe is to *be* the fulfillment of your prayer and to *live* the life style of one who has already attained the result'.[76]

Thankfulness is an essential ingredient of effective prayer, as is silence. Since prayer is a two-way communication system, one who prays must observe a period of meditation or silence to listen for inner guidance or direction.

In a very clear manifestation of African spirituality about which we shall have more to say later in this chapter, Brother Ishmael Tetteh acknowledges the influence of culture in the ways people pray. He singles out for mention and discussion five 'ways of

---

74 Tetteh, *Fountain of Life*, p. 128.
75 Tetteh, *Fountain of Life*, p. 128.
76 Tetteh, *Fountain of Life*, p. 129.

prayer' – affirmation, libation, mental and emotional outpourings, sacrifice and meditation. Moreover, he recognizes and respects various different practices and aids to prayer in the various religious traditions including the burning of candles or incense, use of perfumes, the removal of shoes, clapping of hands, drinking of water, and anointing with oil. He asserts, 'when prayer is understood as a scientific method of harnessing the powers of the mind, feelings and body to experience the absoluteness of God, then any symbol or act that assists in summoning our inner powers is right'.[77]

Meditation is a central act and activity of adherents of the Etherean Mission. Tetteh explains that when we pray we pour out our feelings and thoughts to God. When we meditate we listen to God as God directs us through our souls. Since meditation is a withdrawing from the world and a concentration upon God, and since our experience of the world comes through our senses, meditation requires entry into the 'closet', as recorded in Matthew 6.6. Tetteh interprets this in the following way:

> To enter into your closet is to shut the doors of your outer senses; it is the withdrawal of the five senses (sight, taste, touch, hearing and smell) into inner observation. Man is essentially a spirit being and within his spirit is contained all the wisdom and intelligence of infinite possibilities ... Meditation is the act of withdrawing all of your conscious units to concentrate on the essentials in your life.[78]

Tetteh not only provides the rationale for and explanation of what meditation is he also gives detailed instructions as to how we may meditate. Beginning with the assuming of a comfortable position, breathing deeply, gently and rhythmically, focusing thought through the 'third eye centre' space between the two eyebrows, thinking of the goal of meditation, affirmations and questioning oneself, the devotee is taught how to harness the energy that resides within us all.

---

77 Tetteh, *Fountain of Life*, p. 131.
78 Tetteh, *Fountain of Life*, pp. 137–8.

In addition, he explains and teaches concerning fasting as a necessary discipline that helps in the purification of mind, body and emotions. Spiritual fasts are distinguished from food fasts and also from visual and other fasts. Fasting, for Brother Tetteh, is essentially abstention from anything needed or unnecessary for life, with the clearly focused purpose of intensifying prayer and receiving divine grace. 'Generally', writes Tetteh, 'we fast to create a purified mind, feeling and body in order to be able to retain the spiritual electricity of cosmic Grace (God). Fasting does not make us special before God, but makes us receptive to God's grace.'[79]

On sound: the power of vibration

Brother Ishmael Tetteh sets great store by the value of sound. He argues that the universe is itself a vibrating energy field and that sound is one of the vibrating energies that can be utilized to beneficial ends. Far from being in conflict or competition with science, Tetteh's African mysticism finds great resonance and consonance with science. He cites western scientific method and systems in several places and affirms the findings as in line with divine purpose.[80] Sound affects us positively or negatively. Moreover sound can be used creatively as a tool. Different kinds of music affect us in different ways. But so also, Tetteh argues, does colour and even food, which carries its own vibrational effect on us.

> Sounds bring the spiritual ideas into form. Spirit is pure consciousness; indescribably real. When spirit condenses itself as mind, its earthly correspondence is light while that of feeling is sound. This is easy to identify with because ideas in the mind appear as mental pictures.

---

79 Tetteh, *Fountain of Life*, p. 148.
80 For instance in *The Inspired African Mystical Gospel*, pp. 236–7, Tetteh luxuriates about the anatomy of a cell. He explains in scientific terms that cells breathe, take in food, get rid of waste, grow, reproduce and die and that at the centre of a cell's protoplasm is a nucleus that contains its genetic programme or master plan that controls everything the cell does.

Pictures however, are the play of light in its colors. When the frequency of light reduces it becomes sound and sound becomes form.[81]

Tetteh in advancing the power and utility of vibration and vibrational energy makes reference to mantras, hymns, chants and affirmations, drawing on Indian, Eastern and African mysticism and arguing for the power of healing contained in the right harnessing of sound through these means.

African mystics, Tetteh affirms, believe that it is by a combination of specific vowel sounds that God, the all-pervading spirit, created the entire universe. This he argues is in line with biblical and Christian teaching concerning creation which 'narrates the creation story as God speaking to formlessness or creative darkness and calling forth things into being. This speaking to the "substanceful" darkness is the sounding of words. When sounds are impregnated with thoughts the thoughts manifest.'[82] Tetteh furthers this argument with reference to John's Gospel in the Bible which speaks about the mystical word that was in the beginning with God without which nothing in life was made. 'All things', writes Tetteh, 'are the "fleshification" of the word – the word of God became flesh.'[83] Bringing together the scientific ('sound is vibrational energy') with the spiritual ('God creates the world through sound'), African mystic Tetteh substantiates his teaching:

> Scientifically and spiritually, we know that nothing comes into form without sound. Thoughts are inaudible words or sounds and words are nothing but audible thoughts or sounds. Thought is the realm of the unseen and word is the realm of manifestation.[84]

---

81 Tetteh, *Fountain of Life*, p. 157.
82 Tetteh, *The Inspired African Mystical Gospel*, p. 258. 'Substanceful' is Tetteh's own coinage.
83 Tetteh, *The Inspired African Mystical Gospel*, p. 258. 'Fleshification' is another coining by Brother Tetteh.
84 Tetteh, *The Inspired African Mystical Gospel*, p. 258.

Tetteh thus articulates a very important teaching of African mysticism on the significance of sound: 'Every invention was once just a thought, then by wording it in speech, writing or action, it was created.'[85]

On health and healing: an integrated wholeness

In 2010, the Etherean Mission dedicated a three-floor building in Accra, Ghana, which they had been building for the purposes of health and healing. This building is a holistic hospital to enhance the quality of health and wellbeing for all. The vision of the hospital complex is that when fully operational it will combine African herbal medicine, western allopathic medicine with spiritual (prayer) and mind science for the total well-being of humankind. The ground floor houses the complementary and alternative medicine practitioners, and among others, will be employing the use of herbs, hydrotherapy, massage, yoga, walk therapy and chiropractic therapies. The middle floor houses western allopathic medicine and intends to employ the services of a specialist physician, a gynaecologist and nurses to staff a 45-bed in-patient ward. This floor of the complex also has facilities for surgery. The top floor is the spiritual retreat and 'energization' centre staffed by mystics and spiritual directors that will offer 24-hour unbroken prayer and will use numerous spiritual mind sciences to promote health.

Brother Tetteh identifies five main causes of disease and correspondingly five types of physicians. The causes of disease are (a) astral (b) physiological (c) psychological (d) spiritual and (e) soul causes. By *astral* Tetteh refers to the presence in humanity 'in microcosmic proportions' of the moon, stars, sun and planets.[86] Astral influences are a result of beneficial or else deleterious effects of these cosmic realities acting through their corresponding elements within human beings. Articulating widely held African beliefs, as remedies for these astral diseases, Tetteh suggests, among others, amulets, talismans and baths in water infused with herbs such as

---

85 Tetteh, *The Inspired African Mystical Gospel*, p. 259.
86 Tetteh, *The Inspired African Mystical Gospel*, p. 200.

sunflower and other African herbs which 'are strong with the vibrations of the sun and can therefore counteract the imbalances in the body deriving from the moon and other influences'.[87] With reference to *physiological* causes of illness, Tetteh emphasizes poisonous substances and impurities. Our choice of food is top of his list of attention to prevent disease and promote health. Animals, he argues, refuse to eat or drink things which are injurious to them and select by natural instinct what they require for health. Unfortunately, humans appear most vulnerable to disobedience of their natural instincts and the ingestion and imbibing of that which is injurious in gratification of 'some artificially acquired taste'.[88] Herbal remedies, along with a healthy natural food diet, are recommended to restore and maintain physiological health. *Psychological* causation is the result of states of mind. Such diseases may be caused by 'uncontrolled passions, evil desires, disordered thoughts and morbid imagination . . . self-pity, negative self-image and memory of guilt'.[89] Tetteh here also discusses psychosomatic diseases where the cause is psychological but the effects are physiological. For psychologically caused diseases, as for spiritually caused ones, the remedy proposed is the spiritual counselling approach developed by Brother Tetteh known as 'Soul Processing', which will be presented in the next section. *Spiritual* causation largely results from the evil dispositions of people who will harm and bring destruction upon others. Tetteh argues that our spirits communicate with each other without the use of language. 'If one spirit is angry with another, it may injure him.'[90] Jealousy, envy, vengefulness and wickedness are all mentioned as spiritual disease agents. This is not a matter of intellect for 'spirits are not born from the intellect but from the will'.[91] As remedies Tetteh says, 'absolute knowledge about yourself and your relationship with God and the Cosmos, is the key to your redemption'. However, in cases where the evil will manages to penetrate, 'spiritual baths,

---

87 Tetteh, *The Inspired African Mystical Gospel*, p. 202.
88 Tetteh, *The Inspired African Mystical Gospel*, p. 202.
89 Tetteh, *The Inspired African Mystical Gospel*, pp. 203–4.
90 Tetteh, *The Inspired African Mystical Gospel*, p. 205.
91 Tetteh, *The Inspired African Mystical Gospel*, p. 205.

amulets and prayers are sometimes prescribed to strengthen or increase the force of its psychic shield and thus neutralize the effect of the evil energy'.[92]

For Brother Tetteh, soul caused diseases follow a karmic law. *Soul* causes are those that have not been created by a person in the course of their present life but rather during a former existence. In these cases also, he proposes 'Soul Processing' as a means by which a patient may speed up their process of awareness and giving of themselves to God so as to dissolve ignorance, pain and the 'purgatory of disease'.[93]

Tetteh is at pains to stress that in all cases of disease, whatever the causal forms, 'the physician is only an arm of nature to supply the natural inputs for nature to do her work'.[94] Nature alone is the true healer. The 'major cause of all diseases is ignorance and spiritual awakening is the cure'.[95]

Soul Processing: a path to freedom

Brother Ishmael Tetteh's spiritual quest has been characterized by a desire for practical, proven and workable ways of operationalizing the principles and teachings of the various world religions all of whose precepts he believes are rich with truth. The methods he has used in this quest for practical mysticism have included, 'creative prayer, inner enquiry, observations and investigations of the rationale behind the spiritual and cultural practices of world religions'.[96] Through these means the Etherean Mission, which he describes as 'a spiritual movement that founded itself around me', has developed practical spiritual tools which they describe collectively as EMAT (Etherean Mission Application Technologies).[97] EMAT entail spiritual, social, psychological, physiological and

---

92 Tetteh, *The Inspired African Mystical Gospel*, p. 206.
93 Tetteh, *The Inspired African Mystical Gospel*, p. 207.
94 Tetteh, *The Inspired African Mystical Gospel*, p. 207.
95 Tetteh, *The Inspired African Mystical Gospel*, p. 207.
96 Tetteh, *Soul Processing*, p. 1.
97 Tetteh, *Soul Processing*, p. 1.

financial technologies designed by the Mission for the purposes of achieving balanced living. Tetteh carefully explains EMAT as follows:

> EMAT provides you with workable technologies for harmonious integration and proper functioning of the mind, body and spirit and consequently, gives you the ability to handle life. The goal of EMAT is to make you a free spiritual being with optimum expression . . . Upholding the belief that all knowledge belongs to God, EMAT employs every bit of knowledge considered useful, and these are synthesized into workable technologies for the spiritual, mental and physical well-being of the individual.[98]

EMAT processes include specific practices of meditation, prayer, study, detoxification, touch, isometric and body exercises, breathing exercises, and use of medicinal herbs. *Soul Processing*, described as a 'revolutionary spiritual mind science' lies at the heart of EMAT. 'Soul Processing', says Brother Tetteh, 'deals with the cleansing of the mind of undesirable thoughts and what can stimulate such thoughts, and the activation of the God potential in man.'[99] Soul Processing then is a unique form of spiritual counselling developed by Brother Tetteh which is at the disposal of whoever desires it.

In a book published first in 1985, revised and republished in 1997 and again in 2002, Brother Ishmael Tetteh clearly outlines the processes of Soul Processing and presents several illustrative case studies of clients who have been helped, healed or 'set free' through the process. Soul Processing can be undertaken personally or else with the help and leadership of someone else. The ideal way to practise this form of spiritual counselling is to team up with someone with whom one can comfortably face one's past or current painful incidents. The Etherean Mission has trained persons, called *liberators*, who can be called upon to help with the processing. The *liberator* goes through the painful incident

---

98 Tetteh, *Soul Processing*, p. 2.
99 Tetteh, *Soul Processing*, p. 4.

with the *liberatee* (so called because they are 'on the road to liberty') assisting them with 'non-suggestive questions to experience and re-experience the very painful moments with all' of the perceptions and sense associations contained within it.[100]

A basic premise of Soul Processing is that whatever can be confronted can be handled. As such, in the process a client is led to confront the accumulated pictures of pain and evil that s/he may be living with and to analyse them into constructive learning.[101] Embedded within each painful experience rich learning is believed to exist. Until the learning is realized, the pain repeats itself. It is when the pain is confronted and the learning is absorbed, that the evil in it is dissolved.

Essentially Brother Ishmael Tetteh's form of personal spiritual development which he has called 'Soul Processing' has two parts, namely *Cud Processing* and *Ability Processing*. Cud processing (chewing and removal of the cud) entails 'a gentle process of reliving' in which the origins of present pains are uncovered and reduced through opening persons to the root causes of the pain.[102] Once the primary cause of a specific pain is confronted and removed, the pain and its effects are removed and the individual becomes free. Ability processing, the 'activation of spiritual abilities', then follows. 'It [Ability Processing] is achieved by re-stimulating the pictures of your achievement, successes and your moments of intelligent Christ-like deeds. By focusing on what is divine in you, you expand it.'[103]

Pain, as we have seen, is understood to be a force in opposition to the spirit being's will to be. In moments of pain, the conscious mind which is the spirit being's fountain of expression shuts down, unless the pain can be capably handled by the discriminative faculties of the mind. If it cannot what happens, according to Tetteh, is that it is recorded photographically with all the records of the five senses and filed in the unconscious mind. The unconscious

---

100 Tetteh, *Soul Processing*, p. 59.
101 Tetteh, *Soul Processing*, p. 59.
102 Tetteh, *Soul Processing*, p. 56.
103 Tetteh, *Soul Processing*, p. 56.

mind, as a result, is the repository of all that the conscious mind is unable to deal with immediately. Once filed the pain becomes a law within one's being and can be re-stimulated later through any of the senses associated with the pain. Cud processing entails reliving pains with the express aim of dissolving their power. When a person has been in pain and all the painful perceptions are filed in the unconscious mind, the person through Soul Processing can be encouraged to have enough strength to face and analyse the pain and replay the information. Once all the information is played back to the conscious mind, the discriminating and analysing power within the conscious mind rationalizes and removes the sting from the pain, thereby preventing it from remaining filed.

To further explain and clarify this process, Tetteh employs the concepts of Karma and sin. He argues that the ultimate goal of humans is freedom from karma or sin and the attainment of full enlightenment. Negative karma is the result of pains filed in the unconscious mind. Pain and the conclusions we make in pain determine what experience we need in the future. As such it is past pains, conditions and conclusions that issue in present experiences. The law of karma, Tetteh explains, claims that each of us is here to gain experience and to evolve through many lifetimes towards enlightenment. Mis-experiences or errors result in incarnations to have the opportunity to re-work and correct these errors. Each lifetime though has its own challenges and potential errors. As such it may take thousands of incarnations for enlightenment to be attained. Soul Processing attempts to change those past internal laws and thus change present experiences. As such the advantage of Soul Processing 'is to shorten the time it takes to arrive at your spiritual goals by a billion times'.[104] In short, says Tetteh, 'You are here on the planet to master life. The only way to master life is to master yourself, and Soul Processing gives you that mastery.'[105]

---

104 Tetteh, *Soul Processing*, p. 66.
105 Tetteh, *Soul Processing*, p. 66.

In terms of length of time and the processes of Soul Processing as engaged in through the Etherean Mission, Brother Tetteh asserts:

> Most people experience the full effect of this relief from the third day after a processing session. For cleansing of a whole life therefore, it is advantageous to have about three or more sessions weekly on an evenly spaced time schedule. The average person who is not psychotic or not close to having a psychosis will take an average of one thousand hours to be karma-free. This will be spread over an average of a two-year period. You begin to experience the benefit of Soul Processing right from the first session. Compare this to a billion lifetimes of struggle and uncertainty. Constantly researched techniques are improving the cleansing rate of the technology.[106]

On death and rebirth: changing states of consciousness

Ishmael Tetteh's views on death incorporate elements of thought present in African religions and worldview; Christianity and Hinduism. In African life and thought there are two great events in the life of any human being – birth and death. Birth is the grand entrance into the drama of life on this earth and death is the exit from the scene and re-entry onto the spiritual plane from where one entered at birth. Quoting Ecclesiastes 12.7 and Sirach 14.17, Tetteh argues that when our bodies wear out and are discarded, the spirit continues to live. 'Death', therefore, 'is actually a transition from one state of consciousness to the other. It is a change from physical to spiritual existence. It is simply the release of your physical body into a much freer spiritual life. The physical body wears off and is cast away but the soul, which is indestructible, lives forever.'[107]

Tetteh writes that '[t]he real nature of man is spirit and spirit is eternal'.[108] It is from the Bhagavad Gita that Tetteh finds and quotes

---

106 Tetteh, *Soul Processing*, p. 67.
107 Tetteh, *Fountain of Life*, p. 215.
108 Tetteh, *Fountain of Life*, pp. 214–15.

illustrative support for this view. 'Wise men do not grieve for the dead or living. Never was there a time when I was not, nor you, nor any man, nor will there ever be a time hereafter when we shall cease to be. He who thinks he is slain, and he who thinks he slays, both fail to perceive the real truth; no one either slays or is slain.'[109]

In response to the question where souls go from here after death, Tetteh reveals an important aspect of his understanding. For him, 'death is a change of state of consciousness and not a place. When we die, where we finally settle in the spiritual plane depends on our level of awareness.'[110] He argues that there are different 'planes of existence' each with its sub-planes – the immediate, intermediate and more fine 'astral' planes. Life on the first two of these planes is very much like that on earth, whereas on the astral plane there is not time, neither darkness nor day but rather a clear blue environment. On the astral plane communication is by thought (mind) force alone. Where one finally settles after death depends on one's level of awareness, appetites and spiritual development. People who are 'carnally minded' along with murderers, thieves etc. are gathered together on an astral plane of their own and 'bombard each other with negative thought force and experience pain and torture'. Souls who have led a highly spiritually enriched life 'are drawn to the higher planes where there is peace, serenity and beauty'.[111]

On rebirth, Tetteh argues that being born again is a continuous process of individual transformation in which one grows from the 'son of man' state to the 'son of God' state. It is to be aware of who one is and what one is as spirit. In the 'son of man' state individuals think and feel in myopic ways. They are preoccupied with criticism, shifting blame and condemning others. In the 'son of God' state individuals think cosmically and plan in ways that enhance universal fulfilment and development. In this state one is filled with goodness and is eternal in one's thoughts. Tetteh sees this as not an exclusively Christian thing but rather as being at the core of all religions of the world.

---

109 Tetteh, *Fountain of Life*, p. 215, citing Bhagavad Gita 2.11–19.
110 Tetteh, *Fountain of Life*, p. 222.
111 Tetteh, *Fountain of Life*, p. 223.

The Etherean Mission has formulated a 'Christ Vision' which is for the movement the application and completion of all spiritual laws. The Etherean Mission Christ Vision states:

> See the Good and the Divine or the possible Good and the Divine in yourself and in all of life.

Tetteh comments,

> When you see the good and the divine or the possible good and divine in yourself you will certainly love yourself; similarly, you will love your neighbor. And when you see the good and the divine that life is, you will love it and hold it in sacred reverence; naturally you will love God the source and manifester of Life.[112]

A platform for religious unity

A significant aspect of Brother Ishmael Tetteh's teaching and that of the Etherean Mission is directed towards religious unity. With reference to religious pluralism Tetteh categorically and courageously states: 'I am here to dissolve factionalism and remove barriers and not add to the already saturated life full of barriers.'[113] The *Etherean Mission Handbook* declares, 'The aim of the Etherean Mission is to see a unified universe, which embraces all men [sic] irrespective of race, creed or culture.'[114] There are more quotations and references to the Christian New Testament in the *Handbook* than to any other sacred texts, although Tetteh makes frequent references to the Qur'an and the Bhagavad Gita. Clearly and in proportion to the presence of practitioners of world faiths in Ghana, home of the Etherean Mission, Christianity and African religions are by far the most subscribed to and hence the texts most accessible to adherents of the Etherean Mission. A section of the *Handbook* expresses this thus:

---

112 Tetteh, *Fountain of Life*, p. 234.
113 Tetteh, *The Inspired African Mystical Gospel*, p. 19.
114 Tetteh, *Etherean Mission Handbook*, p. 15.

In Ephesians 4.6 and Acts 10.11–15, 34–35, the Bible teaches that there is only one God within all life and that no matter where you are or who you are, when you do the will of God you are accepted of God. This teaching is about religious oneness and we advocate that.[115]

In a reference reminiscent of Latin American Liberation Theology's advocacy of 'orthopraxy' over orthodoxy as a distinguishing feature of Christian faithfulness, the Etherean Mission asserts, 'Jesus taught, "by their fruits ye shall know them" (Matt. 7.15–16). The proof that a religious teaching is of God is that it produces love, peace, and brotherly [sic] dignity.'[116]

Moreover, the Mission is wary of the 'church that teaches that its brand of religion is the only way to God and that all else are evil' because such teaching bears fruits of conflict, war, fear, separation and hatred. Instead of such narrowness, the Etherean Mission's self-confessed pluralism enriches them 'with great wisdom from all religious traditions'.

In conclusion, and of theological interest and significance is the affirmation within the Mission that 'God has no religion and seeks those who practice love and not those who have the label of a religion'.[117] At once, broadminded and also astute, this controversial statement demonstrates theological depth coupled with ethical directedness. This openness speaks volumes concerning the postcolonializing ethos of the Etherean Mission which is also palpable in their worship and meditational services.

Restoring the mystical traditions of Africa

Without any founders, religious leaders or theologians, with no written texts, propaganda machinery, paid priests or missionaries, African religious beliefs and practices have continued to inspire and influence the lives of countless numbers of people throughout

---

115 Tetteh, *Etherean Mission Handbook*, p. 15.
116 Tetteh, *Etherean Mission Handbook*, p. 15.
117 Tetteh, *Etherean Mission Handbook*, p. 16.

the world. In spite of the absence of these traditional markers of religion, African religious cultures permeate much of continental and diasporan African life, thought and practice. In the face of disparaging renditions, interpretations, classifications, categorizations and the denigration of African traditional religions as evil, archaic, uncouth, demonic and 'pagan', Ishmael Tetteh stands out clearly and declares boldly his allegiance to and indeed vocation to 'the restoration of African mystical religious culture and identity'.[118] Tetteh observes that 'it is interesting to note that at the highest study of metaphysics in any of the organized religions, one ends up recommending the religious principles of Africa'.[119]

Brother Ishmael Tetteh devotes one of his major book publications to the task and aim of the Etherean Mission of restoring the mystical traditions of Africa. The book is titled *The Inspired African Mystical Gospel* and was published in 2001. In one of the most informed, accurate, thoughtful, insightful, creative, original and spiritually attuned pieces of writing I have come across in several years of research on African religions and spirituality, Brother Tetteh not only offers a detailed account of the core beliefs and practices of African religions but also offers interpretations of a wide range of proverbs, wise sayings and symbols from across the continent.

Following an autobiographical account in which he locates himself and his vocation as an African mystic, Brother Tetteh enters upon a deconstructive elucidation of the historic causes of the highly observable negative attitudes of Africans and other world peoples towards African religion. Recognizing that culture and history are what hold a people together giving them a sense of identity and destiny, Tetteh rightly observes: 'The easiest way to destroy a people is to destroy their sense of identity. Unsuspecting Africans cannot see through the very high-powered plan of treachery against them.'[120] Tetteh elaborates on the destruction of African culture and especially the denigration of African religious

---

118 Tetteh, *The Inspired African Mystical Gospel*, p. 9.
119 Tetteh, *The Inspired African Mystical Gospel*, p. 9.
120 Tetteh, *The Inspired African Mystical Gospel*, p. 23.

and spiritual sentiments through derogatory language. He realizes that African religious beliefs are enshrined in African culture and festivals and argues that the onslaught on African cultural practices was aimed at a replacement of the African religious heritage with European derived religion. Tetteh observes how the attacks of Catholic and Protestant missionaries, which to some extent were being retracted, have been taken up with force by the latest wave of Christian ministries. He writes, 'The war on African culture is currently being propagated through the Pentecostal and Charismatic ministries.'[121]

Tetteh points to the widespread and targeted usage of particular pejorative terms to describe various African religious practices which in point of fact are similar to European practices. So, African places of worship are referred to derogatively as 'shrines', while European places are given the more respectable designations as churches or altars. African spiritual leaders are called 'fetish priests/priestesses' while European leaders are accorded the laudatory titles of pastors, reverend ministers, bishops, cardinals and popes. Tetteh continues,

> The African sees God in every atom of creation and therefore worships God in and through rivers, mountains, the sun and the forest. Whilst this is regarded as evil and paganistic, the white man carves a cross out of the forest wood and through it worships God – this is called a crucifix and is revered as divine.[122]

With respect to the African ritual of libation which we discussed briefly in the previous chapter and about which we shall have more to say in this one, Tetteh observes that libation, the African way of praying, is condemned whilst 'breaking bottles of champagne to consecrate a ship is considered normal and divine'.[123] Moreover, and poignantly in regard to devotional and inspirational life, '[R]everence to the ancestors in African worship is

---

121   Tetteh, *The Inspired African Mystical Gospel*, p. 25.
122   Tetteh, *The Inspired African Mystical Gospel*, p. 25.
123   Tetteh, *The Inspired African Mystical Gospel*, p. 25.

considered unholy and evil, however, the calling and reverence of the saints in western religion is considered divine.'[124] Tetteh's concern stems from the pernicious effects of 'mental colonization' which he characterizes as perhaps even worse than the slave trade because it has succeeded in making its victims willing slaves to the colonial power. 'Colonize the mind of a man and you have a willing slave forever.'[125] Tetteh addresses a rallying cry to Africans to 'wake up first to mental freedom':

> To the souls of all Africans I call you to awakening. Rise from the deception and from your long mesmerized sleep. Now is the time for you to pride yourself in what makes you unique as a black race. You have all it takes to make your contribution to world civilization. You are no less than people of other races. In truth we are simply brothers. God creates no junk.[126]

To colonialists, Tetteh also addresses a cautionary word: 'if the colonialists will also awaken to the realization that the destruction of African spirituality and culture is also the destruction of the world's future civilization, they will expedite the recovery of African spirituality'.[127]

Tetteh's appeals stem from his realization that it is by the culture of any peoples that they are identified. And that the destruction of peoples' cultures is the destruction not only of a people's identity but also their spirituality and creativity. 'Destroy the culture of a people and you would have succeeded in destroying their identity. Destroy one's identity and all of his creative ability and hope for happiness is destroyed. The destruction of a culture is the destruction of the thinking and spirituality of a people.'[128] Tetteh argues carefully that the divinity of the spirit of Africa is enshrined in its various cultures. Each African religion is embodied in its culture. The advent of Christianity and Islam into Africa

---

124 Tetteh, *The Inspired African Mystical Gospel*, p. 25.
125 Tetteh, *The Inspired African Mystical Gospel*, p. 27.
126 Tetteh, *The Inspired African Mystical Gospel*, p. 27.
127 Tetteh, *The Inspired African Mystical Gospel*, p. 27.
128 Tetteh, *The Inspired African Mystical Gospel*, p. 28.

went along with a trampling upon of many elaborate and fine cultures. Rich and elaborate African religions and cultures have been destroyed by the sheer ignorance of Europeans and westernized Africans. The gospel shared by western missionaries as well as the faith propagated by Islamists was essentially that everything African was evil and of the devil. Writes Tetteh, '[T]he Bible became an instrument of colonization and still is today. We were told our African names were all evil; African food, dressing, beliefs, medicinal practice, and thinking were all evil. One had to have a white man's name to be holy.'[129] By contrast, Tetteh argues that the British 'were wise enough to establish a British-culture based Christian church', namely the Church of England, 'a new spread of Catholicism based on British cultures, tastes and traditions'.[130] Tetteh is convinced that the main cause of the economic and social woes of Africans lies in the destruction of their culture, identity and spirituality. 'A people who are made to believe that their cultural and spiritual practices are evil, their names are evil and even their skin color is evil are deeply destroyed. The creativity of such people is greatly destroyed.'[131] Recognizing the connectedness between cultural and economic fortunes, Tetteh issues a passionate cry for true emancipation and the decolonizing of the African's spiritual mentality. 'Our economic emancipation is dependent on accepting ourselves for who we are, as unique, beloved and immaculate children of God in our culture.'[132]

The nature of African religion

As has been recorded by many scholars, researchers and observers on Africa, religion is life and life is religion. The African is deeply spiritual. For Africans the spiritual is not separate from

---

129 Tetteh, *The Inspired African Mystical Gospel*, p. 31. As a case in point, my own father had to be given a European name in order to be baptized. In so doing, his African name was changed and as a result to this day I bear a name that is erroneous in terms of my family origin and heritage.
130 Tetteh, *The Inspired African Mystical Gospel*, p. 31.
131 Tetteh, *The Inspired African Mystical Gospel*, pp. 30–1.
132 Tetteh, *The Inspired African Mystical Gospel*, p. 31.

the material. African traditional religion consists of beliefs and practices embodying a complete knowledge system of God, the supreme being, the gods, ancestors, magic, witchcraft, totems, life after death, moral values, destiny and reincarnation. African religious culture is reflected in the daily life style of her people and constitutes the bedrock of politics, marriage, administration, occupation, medicine, and communication. In line with a communitarian ethos, the African is a communal being who practises a communal religion. African religion is developed through the observance of nature and its evolution. Its development has been by the handing down of information by oral tradition from parents to children across generations. Its practices have been invested in spiritual leaders, traditional healers and ritual practitioners who have transmitted their ritual practices to the initiated through ceremonies down through the years. Rituals of birth, puberty, marriage, installation of community leaders and priests, and death, all enshrine and portray in coded form the religious beliefs of Africa.

Tetteh rightly recognizes the pervasive nature of the spiritual perception of traditional African people. All of nature and indeed of life is seen as expressive of the divine. God is entwined with all that exists, seen or unseen. 'The African sees nature as the embodiment of God. Great reverence is given to life in a holistic manner. There is only one life expressed in various forms and this life is God.'[133] Observing and respecting nature is observing and showing respect for God. Nature, and all life which is in fact an expression of nature, embodies and reflects God.

Monotheism and polytheism

Brother Ishmael Tetteh presents a mystical view of the subject of the number of divine entities recognized and worshipped in African religion which is exactly the same as was offered me during my research with an Akan traditional healer-priestess. This is how Tetteh puts it:

---

133 Tetteh, *The Inspired African Mystical Gospel*, p. 256.

African mystical worship and celebrations advocate a Supreme Being beyond all that is, and ever shall be. Africans do not see any conflict in worshipping and adoring aspects of this one Supreme Being. To them, monotheism and polytheism are only various standpoints of observing the same thing. In monotheism you see the singular as all things and in polytheism you see 'the all things' that form the body of the singular. Between the two stands there truly is no conflict whatsoever.[134]

According to Tetteh, African mystics regard the Supreme Being as a unified whole with many different aspects. The monotheistic religions in the world, on this view, worship one or other of the aspects of this Oneness that they erroneously consider and enforce as absolute and exclusive. Religious wars have been the result of such reductionism. Africans may fight tribal or ethnic wars but do not traditionally fight over or on behalf of gods or religion.

On this theme, in response to my question, 'How many gods are there? How many do you call upon?', an Akan traditional healer-priestess replied, 'Do you think counting is relevant? Can you count in spiritual terms?' She went on to explain that counting and numbering is a very earthly game. On the spiritual plane it has no meaning or significance. One, 44, 77, these all have no significance when applied to the spiritual realm. To her counting is merely a human way of trying to appropriate the complexity of the spiritual, divine realm.

The nature of God: African mystical theology

For an African sense of the nature of the Ultimate God, Brother Tetteh asks that we listen to the names by which God is referred to in the various African languages. In this book, Tetteh draws upon names of God among the Gã, Akan, Ewe, Yoruba and Mende peoples of West Africa to illustrate the nature of the divine.

To the Gã, as previously indicated, God is referred to as Ataa Naa Nyɔŋmɔ which, as Tetteh correctly indicates, means Father

---

[134] Tetteh, *The Inspired African Mystical Gospel*, p. 35.

(*Ataa*) Mother (*Naa*) Visitor of the Dawn (*Nyɔŋmɔ*). As 'visitor of the dawn' God is known as the silent creative presence behind the senses. Mother-Father speaks of the bisexual, dual nature of the ultimate presence as a 'supernal Father and Mother'.[135]

To the Akan, God is *Onyame* (that which satisfies) and *Twereduampon* (the large and strong tree upon which one can lean without it getting bent). God then is known to the Akan as the desire and fulfilment, at the deepest soul level, of every human craving. God is also the support and sustainer of life, the tree of life. Moreover, God is *Onyankopon* (the Great or bosom friend), the never failing presence.

Ewe names of God referred to include *Mawu* (Almighty One), *Mawunyo* (God is kind) and *Wola* (Creator). From the Yoruba Tetteh refers to *Olorun Olore* (God the benefactor), *Olukoya* (the Lord who champions the cause of the suffering) and *Yataa* (the One whom you meet everywhere). From the Mende people of Sierra Leone, he points to *Ngewo* (the Great Spirit) and *Leve* (the High up one).

Brother Tetteh explains that the African traditionally acknowledges that there is ultimately one life and one spiritual presence. However, the creator is not separate from the creation and noticing that without the earth, water, sunlight and air the seed will not grow concludes that the one life that is God is revealed as these four elements, and more. Veneration of God is therefore sometimes channelled through these elements. 'The river god, the sun god, the earth god and the god of the air are all aspects of the one presence of God.'[136] God is known to be revealed through earthly and heavenly bodies such as the sky, moon stars, rain, trees, rivers and seas. God is within them and yet transcends them all.

The Ultimate God is not worshipped directly. The Ultimate Supreme Being has no shrines, temples or altars. The Ultimate One is way too enormous for such. S/he is approached normally through divinities who act as intermediaries. God is invoked directly on very special occasions or in great crises and only by

---

135 Tetteh, *The Inspired African Mystical Gospel*, p. 39.
136 Tetteh, *The Inspired African Mystical Gospel*, p. 41.

the appropriate agents. God, however, is the ultimate recipient of all worship. Though they cannot worship God directly, everyone has direct access. The Akans, for instance, say 'if you wish to say something to God whisper it to the wind'.

Gods, messengers, or sons and daughters?

Concerning the so-called 'gods', 'deities' or 'divinities' Brother Ishmael Tetteh articulates the belief of many practitioners of African religions. My own research with practitioners, priest-healers and diviners in West Africa bears him out and demonstrates the misapprehension of many foreign scholars and writers on African religion who appear to have been more anxious to replicate other western scholars or else confirm theories devised by westerners than they have been to listen to or accept the faith of the African practitioners themselves.[137] In this African way of reckoning, the Ultimate is the great creator, the author of and power behind the entire universe. God is the sustainer of the universe, the one who provides air, water and sunlight; the supreme source of all life. The Ultimate One is omnipotent, omnipresent, omniscient, eternal, self-caused, self-existent, kind, merciful and generous. God is the source of all moral laws and codes. God maintains these laws which give painful or joyful results in accordance with human action. God is the discerner and knower of all

---

137 See Emmanuel Lartey, *Pastoral Counselling in Inter-cultural Perspective*, Frankfurt/London/New York: Peter Lang, 1987, pp. 70–7. My contention there on the basis of painstaking research is that a better category for the understanding of the place of African 'gods' – one that is more true to the actual beliefs of Africans – is that of 'messengers, angels or spirits' rather than 'deities or gods'. The place of the 'gods' as messengers of the Ultimate is what I heard expressed and understood from practitioners again and again. The notion that 'gods' are ultimate in themselves propagated by western scholars and Christian apologists seeking to interpret African beliefs in western categories is simply erroneous. This way of categorizing the African religious universe has led to much misunderstanding and mis-characterizing of African religious practice in relation to these deities. They most certainly are not 'demons' or 'evil spirits' as Christians have been taught to consider them. To the practitioners of African religion they are sons, daughters and messengers from God.

human hearts. God is the all-seeing and all-knowing one before whom nothing is hidden or secret. As such no shrine or temple made by human hands is fitting for such a One as this.

Tetteh expresses what correctly characterizes the 'gods' as follows:

> God rules through his own divine ideas embodied as the gods of life. God has legions of gods (divine ideas) under him, which present themselves in rocks, trees and rivers and through all life forms. The gods are the sons and daughters of the most high God with specific responsibilities.[138]

African mystical theology affirms that the one life that God is expresses as all life forms. Each life form is a divine idea in expressive form. Brother Tetteh refers to a conversation he had with an African mystic in which she offered the following analysis of the Supreme Being as head of the state and the (demi) gods as ministers (secretaries) of state:

> You do not go to the president for penicillin when you have an infection but you rather go to the minister [secretary] of health or doctor if your medical needs have not been addressed . . . God in his own wisdom has democratically decentralized himself so that it will be easy for us to reach to our needs under the offices [gods] he has instituted.[139]

In many African cultures, the earth itself is a living presence, a great 'god' for the people. Because of its evidently motherly nature, the earth is considered the wife of the Ultimate God or else the female aspect of God. She discerns and knows the mind and 'secrets' of the Ultimate. The earth itself is a great spiritual power, the supreme mother and queen mother of all nations. 'Her holy presence is found in every woman', Tetteh declares.[140] Among the Asante

---

138 Tetteh, *The Inspired African Mystical Gospel*, p. 44.
139 Tetteh, *The Inspired African Mystical Gospel*, p. 47.
140 Tetteh, *The Inspired African Mystical Gospel*, p. 45.

peoples and also many other African peoples, the queen mother has the sole right and responsibility to elect a person to be chief or traditional ruler. The earth as mother is the sacred womb from which men were begotten and to whom they will return. 'For this reason', says Tetteh, 'her permission is sought in prayers, libation and sacrifices before a grave is dug.' The earth goddess is revered. Festivals are held in her honour and many ethnic groups have dedicated sacred days of the week to her. Tetteh goes on to explain that the great goddess of the earth is the queen of the gods and is the goddess of fertility and owner of the lands. The earth is and must therefore be regarded as sacred. This explains the various prayer and libation rituals that are engaged in traditionally prior to hunting, sacrifices, the felling of trees or carving of drums from trees. Tetteh states, 'The earth goddess is the initiator and protector of public and private morality. She hates falsehood, stealing, murder, incest, adultery and sex in the bush or on the bare ground.'[141]

The sum of the matter is clear. The gods or divinities are sons and daughters brought into being by the Ultimate God. The 'gods' do not have self-existence. They derive their powers from the Ultimate God the Creator and Source of all Life. God has given each 'god' an administrative role in God's theocratic world government. The 'gods' in African thought then serve the same purpose as angels do in Christianity and Islam. They play the roles of God's ministers, messengers, linguists, children and intermediaries. Says Tetteh,

> To call upon the name Orisha-nla (Yoruba god of sculpture) Orisha-oko (Yoruba god of agriculture and fertility) and Shango (god of justice) is to call upon God's spiritual energy of sculpturing, agriculture and fertility and of justice respectively. The gods are the embodied divine ideas of God. To know the gods is to know the divine ideas of God and embody them.[142]

---

141 Tetteh, *The Inspired African Mystical Gospel*, p. 45.
142 Tetteh, *The Inspired African Mystical Gospel*, p. 49.

God, the Ultimate, has given to humankind 'gods' (deities) to guide us, in order that through embracing and receiving them human beings may receive God's infinite divine attributes. Tetteh explains that there are nature gods, medicine gods and gods that express the various attributes of the divine. There are also 'deified ancestors' who he also names as 'ascended beings'. These ancestors were persons of great spirituality, medical knowledge and prowess, or founders of clans and towns. All – gods and ancestors – are revered because they reveal and manifest aspects of the mystery and wisdom of the One Divine Essence that permeates all of life and nature.

Brother Ishmael Tetteh succeeds in conveying an inner essence of the African religious views which, as I have indicated previously, articulates beliefs and practices that I found to be the case in my research with African traditional priest-healers. An important aspect of this is to be found in the African practitioners' views concerning the world and the universe as a whole. Brother Tetteh expresses this in the following way:

> African mystics believe that the universe is the body of God and that everything, seen or unseen, is there to reveal an attribute or spiritual quality of God.[143]

This sense of the connectedness of natural world with the Divine makes for a deep understanding of the sacrality of the universe and reverence for all that exists – a hallmark of African religions and spirituality. Drawing on and elaborating this belief Tetteh utilizes a solar and lunar analogy drawing out its practical and ritual significance in African mystical practice. The sun and moon are understood as consorts. The sun is revered as a prime mover, custodian and creator of all things on earth. The moon has a tempering effect on the energy of the sun, regulating the energy the sun brings to the earth. Towards the end of each year, in December, the sun receives special energies from Father-Mother God and from the stars and other heavenly bodies. The heavenly

---

143 Tetteh, *The Inspired African Mystical Gospel*, p. 229.

bodies are all living beings that bestow blessings on human beings (as children of God). The earth receives cosmic energy and life from the universe through the sun. African mystics as such perform rituals to be in resonance with the sun and the moon. Tetteh refers to a prayer ritual that is performed for twenty-eight days for a woman and twenty-nine days for a man. The reason for this particular number of days is that the earth absorbs one divine idea at the completion of one circulation of the moon around the earth. Tetteh explains, 'the number of days it takes the female to assimilate a divine idea is twenty-eight because the female is known as the balanced one, while the male is known as the unbalanced one and therefore must perform the rituals for twenty-nine days'.[144] These mystics further believe that several diseases are the result of imbalance of the sun and moon energies and as such employ herbal treatments that are reservoirs of solar or lunar energies.

The ancestors: illustrious 'ascended geniuses'

Recognition, veneration and honouring of the illustrious dead is a central feature of African religion. In fact, for Anthony Ephirim-Donkor, following a most detailed and in-depth study of the Akan people of Ghana, 'African religion is ancestor worship'.[145] Serving as 'the invisible police force of the family and community' those who having lived worthy lives and made significant contributions to the well-being of the human community while they lived, and who have now died and passed on to the unseen realm, 'are the harmonious bridge between the living world and the supernatural world'.[146] It is through them that the spirit world becomes real to the living. Their spiritual presence is understood to assist in the settling of disputes. They are called upon to act as witnesses to

---

144 Tetteh, *The Inspired African Mystical Gospel*, p. 233.
145 Anthony Ephirim-Donkor, *African Religion Defined: A systematic study of ancestor worship among the Akan*, New York/Toronto/Plymouth: University Press of America, 2013, p. vii.
146 Tetteh, *The Inspired African Mystical Gospel*, p. 272.

TRANSCENDING COLONIAL RELIGION

any serious commitments and promises made by the living to seek harmony and well-being between and among communities. They are revered as the leaders and moral exemplars of the good life for the living community. They offer advice, warnings and information for successful living through dreams and the divinations of seers and prophets. They are believed to be the unseen presence that presides over family gatherings and which therefore serves to bind families together. Ancestors are the symbols and spirits of unity and social solidarity for families and communities.

Ancestors are arbiters of morality who give and enforce the moral code of the community. They expedite fulfilment for those who abide by the moral code and also bring corrective punishment on those who disobey. Their presence is invoked at all important social gatherings, because they are seen as the link between the past and the present. They act therefore as the bond of cohesion of the society, and the means and mediators of the continual link between the human and the divine realms.

Tetteh, in postcolonial vein as other African religionists have as well, argues for the similarity between the cult of the ancestors and the Christian 'communion of saints' pointing out how the African practice is denigrated while the European Christian version is praised and lauded. Tetteh comments, 'people without ancestors are people without souls'.[147] He is convinced that one's psychic or spiritual power increases by the number of people one is in harmony with. Tetteh therefore offers rituals for harnessing ancestral power: 'You are made strong by your line of ancestors, and by blessing the good in them you are blessing your very source and establishing yourself in goodness.'[148]

Libation: quintessential African form of prayer

Among the Gãs, the Akans and many other people groups in Africa, the giving of a drink, usually water, to a guest is a sign of welcome, recognition, acknowledgement and thanks for visiting.

---

147 Tetteh, *The Inspired African Mystical Gospel*, p. 272.
148 Tetteh, *The Inspired African Mystical Gospel*, p. 274.

If a guest is not recognized by the serving of a drink, it is an indication that one is not welcome and must leave. Considering the names for God of the people groups we have referred to God is seen as a personal visitor, a divine presence and a great and intimate friend. The logic of symbolism which follows this recognition is that presence of God is to be acknowledged and welcomed through the pouring of a drink. Now, since the earth is the divine consort and God is one with the earth, with water and with air, fire and the elements of life, 'pouring libation unto earth or to any of the other elements with the focus prayer on God is perfectly divine'.[149] Pouring of libation is the quintessential mode of prayer in traditional Africa and arises out of the culture of hospitality and recognition.

Prayer is accompanied by different gestures, body postures and positioning in different religious and cultural settings. Moslems sit on the ground and touch their foreheads to the earth. Prostrating, kneeling, closing one's eyes, clasping one's hands together and other bodily acts symbolize piety, devotion and sacred intent in different cultures. So also in African traditional cultures the pouring of drink on the earth accompanied by particular forms of words is a sacred way of symbolizing prayer focus and intent.

Brother Ishmael Tetteh finds examples of the pouring of drink offerings in the Bible and notes that these serve as indications that there is no divine objection to the practice, but rather divine injunction. In Genesis 28.18, the patriarch Jacob rises early in the morning and pours oil on the stone he had used as a pillow and which had been the site of his heavenly dream in which God had spoken to him. This act also served to consecrate the place of which Jacob had declared, 'How awesome is this place! This is none other than the house of God and the gate of heaven' (Gen. 28.16), and as a sign of the change of the name from Luz to Bethel (i.e. house of God). Jacob returns there again later in his journeying at the command of God and 'poured out a drink offering on it (the stone) and poured oil on it' (Gen. 35.14). Further, among the daily offerings Yahweh instituted for the Israelites given to them through Moses was a

---

149 Tetteh, *The Inspired African Mystical Gospel*, p. 207.

'drink offering [which] shall be one-fourth of a hin for each lamb'. God commanded the people: 'In the Holy Place you shall pour out a drink offering of strong drink to the LORD' (Num. 28.7). Tetteh argues that these and other biblical examples serve to offer guidance to 'stimulate and liberate higher thinking' and thus to encourage practitioners in the rituals of libation.[150]

The usual traditional form of libation prayer rituals begin with an officiant having water or an alcoholic drink in hand. He or she first raises the drink to the skies addressing the Supreme ultimate God with words such as 'God Almighty, we show you drink but we do not presume to give you, the source of all that is, drink'. Next follows the pouring of a portion of the drink on the earth in acknowledgement of Mother Goddess Earth. Then the deities are recognized with another act of pouring and this is followed by the ancestors being named with the pouring of some more drink. The named ancestors are implored to in turn call upon their unnamed ancestors and cause there to be an invocation and realization that reverberates throughout the entire cosmos on the spiritual plane. Finally the one praying declares an intention, request or desire and ends with a thanksgiving for the audience of all who have been called upon in this act of prayer.

The art and practice of libation embodies cultural, religious, and ethical beliefs that are widely shared by African peoples. It could very well be a cultural vessel through which the essence of prayer in all its forms can be conveyed and practised. I see nothing wrong with taking this form and investing it with the language and verbal expressions that convey the understanding of the divine that is sought.

African traditional medicine and healing; a spiritual science

The practice of healing is an integral aspect of the traditional function of African priests and priestesses within the community. Traditionally, every problem is a spiritual one at core. Disease is essentially defined 'as a shift from spiritual equilibrium and its

---

150 Tetteh, *The Inspired African Mystical Gospel*, p. 208.

treatment hinges on bringing the individual as composite of mind, feeling and body in harmony with his/her spirit'.[151] The spirit is the upright, perfect and unsullied essence of a human person. Illness is a transgression of the mind, emotions or body against the spirit. As such healing of any disease may require, together with other things, 'pacifications of the spirit and a change in one's attitude so that the spirit is no more offended'.[152] In African traditional medical practice, then, much attention is paid to the spirituality of the patient. The medical practitioner themselves must also inspire faith and connect spiritually with the patient for healing to be effected.

In terms of remedies that are offered it is important to understand that Africans traditionally believe that we inhabit a spiritual universe and that everything, including plants and herbs, have a spiritual essence. In gathering plants and herbs for medicinal purposes, the practitioner must first recognize the particular spiritual life-giving force with which each plant or herb is imbued. African literary genius and wordsmith Ayi Kwei Armah captures this traditional healing science in his insightful book *The Healers*. In response to the child Densu's question about what traditional healers see and hear in the forest Armah has the healer Damfo respond:

> Say the snake bites a child. Those who walk through the forest with their ordinary eyes see the child near death, lying there helpless in the middle of all the leaves of the forest. The healer sees not just a mass of leaves. He can recognize the different spirit in each kind of leaf. He can see the leaf that has a spirit opposite to, and stronger than, the snake's poison. He can squeeze out its juice for the spirit contained in it and use it to save the child. You see, it is as if the spirits of all the leaves of the forest were talking to the healer, telling him what it is they contain, what it is each can do, and what they cannot do. The leaves, animals, even stones say much, and they show much, to any prepared to see and hear.[153]

---

151 Tetteh, *The Inspired African Mystical Gospel*, p. 234.
152 Tetteh, *The Inspired African Mystical Gospel*, p. 234.
153 Ayi Kwei Armah, *The Healers: A Novel*, Popenguine, Senegal: Per Ankh, 2000, p. 94.

African mystics, Tetteh argues, declare that plants are living beings with full ability to hear and respond to spiritual and physical stimuli. As such they must be treated with respect as living beings through whom God gives healing. Respect to the healing power of the plant is respect to God. 'The African mystic does not see a plant life separate from God's life. There is but one life of God expressed in all things and as all things.'[154]

African mystical practice: 'the magic is in the practice'

In all his books, Brother Ishmael Tetteh offers readers exercises and practices by which the truths he writes about can become real in their own lives. Brother Tetteh presents an African mystical practical theology which draws very heavily on the practices of African traditional priest healers, African religious and spiritual traditions, and his own practices of mysticism. *The Inspired African Mystical Gospel* is no exception. Here he has chapters not only on African philosophy and theology but also on African spirituality, sacred prayers and songs, aphorisms and proverbs, stories, naming ceremonies, marriage, puberty rites, death and ministry to the dead, widowhood rites, rites for consecration of land and stools (i.e. thrones for chiefs), festivals, medicine and healing, ancestral power and African symbols. The text is laced with thoughtfully crafted ritual practices which embody the beliefs that lie deeply buried within African religious and spiritual teaching. In Brother Tetteh and the Etherean Mission we have the hallmarks of a genuinely postcolonializing African spiritual movement.

---

154 Tetteh, *The Inspired African Mystical Gospel*, p. 235.

5

Postcolonializing Pastoral Care

My personal journey as a pastoral caregiver and pastoral theologian has followed the trajectory I mapped out as discernible in the global history of these disciplines.[1] Beginning with my training and early practice which can be understood as squarely within the 'globalization' paradigm in which regardless of origins one learned western models as normative and in point of fact as the only acceptable ways of engaging people pastorally, I entered into an 'internationalization' phase. As a practitioner and teacher, I prepared students and practised pastoral care and counselling following a paradigm I describe as internationalization in which some attention is paid to cultural diversity in a 'cross-cultural' manner. Respect is paid to other approaches and there is an attempt at dialogue between the different culturally preferred ways of attending to the needs and concerns of persons. A major handicap of these internationalist ways of working is the power and legitimacy imbalance between the 'western' and the 'other' approaches. In my experience of actual practice, the western ways inevitably prove dominant, with the other ways being seen as exotic at best, unprofessional at worst. More recently, I have embraced a paradigm of 'indigeneity' with enthusiasm and found within the local knowledge of postcolonial subalterns much that is therapeutically very significant, with a great deal to counterbalance my westernized biases. As has by now become clear, I believe the models,

---

1 See my chapter, Emmanuel Lartey, 'Globalization, Internationalization and Indigenization of Pastoral Care and Counseling', in Nancy Ramsey (ed.), *Pastoral Care and Counseling: Redefining the Paradigms*, Nashville: Abingdon, 2004, pp. 87–108.

reflections and practices I write about and currently advocate reflect very much those of indigenous African practitioners of the African traditional arts of spiritual care and reflective healing practice.

In the turn from a globalizing towards an indigenizing pastoral methodology, African pastoral caregiving has occasionally moved under the impetus of a postcolonializing ethos. In this postcolonializing practical theology the central understanding of pastoral care is that it is a double-edged sword with cutting surfaces that are community-building and culture-transforming. The handle of this dual cutting edge device which makes it possible to wield it effectively is the incorporation of spirituality.

The centrality of spirituality

At the core of African anthropologies lies a central organizing aspect of the human personality variously designated (e.g. Akan *okra*; Gã *kla*; Ancient Egyptian *ka*; Yoruba *ori*), which refers to a God-given essence that is received or uniquely chosen from the divine realm prior to entry onto the earth plane, and that serves as the core or key driving force of a human being's life purpose, character or personality. This component of one's personality links one with the divine while also being the core of one's psychology. African traditional healers and diviners locate their activities very often centrally in this aspect of a human's being. Any approaches to the care of persons within an African environment that does not address this central feature, or that has nothing to offer that dimension of a person's experience, is fundamentally flawed and doomed to failure. Pastoral caregivers within such social and cultural spaces are called upon to engage this 'spiritual' element if their work is to scratch where their clients itch. When great psychological theories (and the therapeutic practices that follow from them) do not recognize that spirituality is central to the personality of Africans, they essentially suffer this failure.

Postcolonializing pastoral care within African social environments (including African diasporan spaces) finds ways of challenging the psychological reductionism of westernized approaches to pastoral care and counselling. Postcolonializing pastoral care centres spirituality integrally and crucially. Spirituality instead of psychology becomes the major cognate discipline for pastoral care. However 'spirituality', understood in the African sense I am discussing, is a synthetic concept. Postcolonializing approaches re-adopt this African sense and engage the spiritual essence of persons, recognizing that this essence has divine as well as psychological, social and ecological dimensions to its complexity. While privileging the divine, these approaches explore the interrelationships between the divine, the psychological, the sociological and the ecological. (By ecological I mean relations with the natural world – the earth, geographical features such as rivers, rocks, mountains; the flora and fauna; and the world of animals.) Postcolonializing pastoral care then is about helping persons fulfil the life-purpose and plan they chose and agreed to in the divine realm prior to their birth and entry onto this human plane of existence. It is about discerning and utilizing their 'spirituality' to navigate the issues of their life successfully in ways that will contribute to the well-being of the human community.

Building healthy community

Postcolonializing pastoral care is about community building. A central motivation for these approaches to pastoral care is a communal relational one. One of the downsides of the drive for the autonomous, self-directed, personally morally-responsible, rational, logic-centred, individual envisaged and imposed by the westernizing colonial social agents was the loss of community and the socially and relationally integrated persons that traditional African morals upheld. I am not arguing for one to replace the other which sadly was the effect of colonialism. Had there been a greater respect for the communal values of the colonized a better balance would have been sought between the rugged rational individual and the socially responsible communal person. As it was, pastoral care, as is still the case in many westernized contexts, was equated with pastoral counselling. Individual therapy became the defining model of pastoral care and all forms of care were examined at the bar of their effectiveness in satisfying the emotional needs of individuals. Increasingly, thankfully, it is being recognized that true pastoral care creates communities within which acts of care and counselling have meaning and significance. Pastoral practices and pastoral counselling, whether by 'professional' or untrained caregivers, are the natural outflow of these communities of care. Healthy communities – like healthy families – produce healthy people. Individuals who receive excellent therapy and whose inner lives are repaired only to return into unwholesome social circumstances will soon be re-infected and need to return for individual therapy. It is the growth of healthy societies that will lead to the stabilization of healthy persons. An individual cannot be well in a sick society. In any case, there is the need for attention both to the care of individuals and the care of communities, if there is to be an encompassing delivery of health.

The aim of postcolonializing pastoral care is the cultivation of communal spaces in which all people can be safe, nurtured and empowered to grow. The focus on individual therapy to the exclusion of communal care follows the pattern of an ineffectual colonialism. Individual therapy itself is set within a community building paradigm that privileges the growth of persons as social beings and communal participants who seek the well-being of total groups. Pastoral caregivers, by virtue of their recognition of the importance of communal space and communal resources, will be in the forefront of the struggle for safety in community. They will seek to establish places of safety for all persons at risk of molestation, violence, discriminatory or oppressive practices of any sort. This will mean a keen eye for potential danger evident in the social climate. Aware of the fact that societies can be manipulated and mobilized in ways that oppress minority groups, they will be searching through social and public policy making processes for any hints of legislation that could prove harmful to certain groups. They will in such instances be willing to organize against such policies ever becoming law.

They will be mobilizing resources for the provision of safe houses for women at risk of violence, and the staffing of such premises with suitably trained personnel. They will be engaging in the political processes of the communities in which they are in the interest of disadvantaged and marginalized groups. This means that a crucial part of the pastoral caregiver's art is listening for the voices of the marginalized of whatever kind. Such voices are frequently very loud by their absence, so pastoral caregivers will be attuned to the voices of the silenced and the silence of the voiceless. Pastoral caregiving includes advocacy for social justice, and pastoral givers do not shy away from participating in and engaging the political process in the interest of the creation of humane communities. The goal of pastoral care is always the creation of healthy communities in which *all persons* can live humane lives.

Human dignity is premised upon social institutions and processes of nurture and growth. Institutions such as schools and hospitals are established with the express purpose of providing for these processes. Pastoral caregivers participate in such institutions as chaplains, teachers, social workers and pastors. In their function as pastoral caregivers they view their presence as not merely the provision of a vaguely defined 'spiritual' care but rather that of seeking the total dignity and well-being of all persons within and affected by these institutions.

Transforming cultures

Ultimately, postcolonializing pastoral care has to do with the transformation of cultures. Pastoral care really functions as a postcolonializing and therefore liberating human activity, in line with divine practice, when it aims at changing underlying assumptions about human communities, about divine presence and activity, and about human well-being. Accordingly pastoral care aims not merely at the personal transformation of individuals, but rather at changing the total ecology of the world, the nature of relations between and amongst peoples. Communities, and therefore individuals, are set within cultures. Whole cultures can promote and maintain healthy communities which in turn nurture individuals who are well. Cultures, in which the signs, symbols, tendencies, ideologies and covert assumptions are disrespectful of human persons and death-dealing, cannot produce healthy communities. Communities that result from the postcolonializing pastoral care activities and practices referred to do bear the hallmarks and characteristics of health, safety and human dignity, interpersonal, communal and inter-communal well-being.

Institutional chaplains, in hospitals, schools, military or industry, are particularly faced with the challenge of transforming cultures. This is because they are called upon to care for the ethics and modus operandi of whole institutions. It is a role of an institutional chaplain to inquire about the extent to which the culture of their institution serves the well-being of the people within them and the people they serve. Counselling individuals and families is a part of an institutional chaplain's role. Organizing for the religious rites and rituals that are needed in times of loss, transition or celebration is most certainly a chaplain's job. Creating wholesome communal activities and spaces for the rejuvenation and spiritual recreation of all within the institution falls frequently to the chaplain. However, the institutional chaplain's function becomes most crucial and called for when the culture of their institution militates against the well-being of particular groups within the institution, when a culture of disrespect, abuse, bullying or ignoring of the rights, needs and concerns of any persons associated with the institution creeps into play.

6

Postcolonializing God: A Theological Imperative

Sɛ nnipa nyinaa soa Nyankopɔn a, obiakofo nnuru mu afu.[1] (Akan)

On a social level the Akan saying quoted above appeals to people, rather like the English 'many hands make light work', to band together to make any task easier by sheer virtue of it being shared. The choice of images in the Akan, though, is intriguing. Nyankopɔn, as we have seen, is an Akan name for God. So a literal translation of the proverb is 'when all people carry God, no one person becomes hunchbacked'. The picture is fascinating – a large group of people carrying God! The theological insight is incredible. When only one person or group of persons 'carries God' the burden is intolerable and they become hunchbacked. The onerous duty of 'carrying God' is best done by many groups of people working together.

Christian theology has been done predominantly utilizing tools and resources developed in European contexts. By application of the Akan wise saying this inadequate sharing of the tasks of theology has resulted in a European hunchback. Moreover, by that same token, a distortion of the understanding of God has resulted. The erasure of an aspect of the image of God in humanity has led to a warped picture of the nature of God. Having been forced to exclude the African, and other peoples, from the construction of the image of God, Christians have been made to see God exclusively in European terms. This has meant that we have been restricted to only one aspect of the divine mystery. Postcolonial analysis of particularly western Christian formulations that were

---

1 Translation into English: 'When the whole world (i.e. all people) makes God its burden, none (no one person) becomes hunchbacked.'

transmitted and imposed on African peoples suggests that we have been made to worship a European crafted 'idol' – a creation made in the image of the philosophies, anthropologies, intellectual and emotional preferences of Europeans to fit their felt needs and provide remedies for their foibles. This 'idol' has taken the place of the God of all creation whose manifold wisdom, infinite majesty and ineffable mystery can only be glimpsed through the collective image of all humanity. It is the whole of humanity that is 'the image of God', created in reflection of the Creator God. As such, forcibly removing or else deliberately ignoring the reflection, understanding and contribution concerning the nature of God from any part of humanity results in a very impoverished, lopsided and inadequate vision of the divine. A significant reflection on this situation from the African perspective is voiced by Brother Ishmael Tetteh,

> Africa has a contribution to make to world civilization. She is to provide spiritual civilization. It is only when Africa has arisen and made its vital spiritual contribution that the world will see true civilization on the planet. It demands everyone, white, pink, yellow and coloured to contribute towards the restoration of African spirituality. The African problem is the problem of humanity. Let Africa sink and we will all sink. Colonize the thinking of Africa and you will only succeed in colonizing and destroying the wisdom and the spiritual light of the world.[2]

Mimicry

A strategy often adopted by the colonized as well as in the discourse of post-Enlightenment English colonialism is that of mimicry. Homi Bhabha, focusing on the latter, analyses colonialism's literary adoption of the ambivalent power of the farce or comical. 'Mimicry', writes Bhabha, 'emerges as one of the most elusive and

---

2 Ishmael N. O. Tetteh, *The Inspired African Mystical Gospel*, Accra: Etherean Mission Publishing, 2001, p. 26.

effective strategies of colonial power and knowledge'.[3] Bhabha recognizes the forked tongue in several colonialist depictions such as of the translator, the colonial politician as play-actor and the partial imitator.[4] The irony in these 'authorized versions of otherness' Bhabha sees as demonstrating the essence of colonial mimicry. For 'colonial mimicry is the desire for a reformed, recognizable Other, *as a subject of a difference that is almost the same, but not quite*'.[5] Such ambivalence provides the justification for continued surveillance because of the inappropriateness, incompleteness and virtualness with the colonial subject that it points to. 'The success of colonial appropriation depends on a proliferation of inappropriate objects that ensure its strategic failure, so that mimicry is at once resemblance and menace.'[6] Bhabha argues that 'the menace of mimicry is its double vision which in disclosing the ambivalence of colonial discourse also disrupts its authority'.[7] So while it is important that the colonized be as much 'the same' as the colonizer as possible, this sameness must always be qualified – 'almost... but not quite'. Meanwhile, intriguingly, this dissimilarity, this double vision, is both necessary and menacing.

In my experience the colonized adopted the mimetic strategy to fulfil both objectives. On the one hand being able to reproduce the colonizer's activities 'to the letter' made clear to the colonizer that the colonized, far from being incapable, incompetent or even subhuman, actually possessed all the capabilities of the colonizer. On the other hand mimicry, because it always contained an element of mockery, remained menacing to the colonizer, always causing uncertainty as to what the colonized was actually trying to convey and ominously suggesting that the colonized may actually have had an edge over the colonizer. The colonized could 'play the part', which meant he or she knew and lived a different life inaccessible to the colonizer, while also knowing what the colonizer knew,

---

3 Homi K. Bhabha, *The Location of Culture*, London/New York: Routledge, 1984, p. 85.
4 Bhabha, *Location of Culture*, p. 86.
5 Bhabha, *Location of Culture*, p. 86. Italics in the original.
6 Bhabha, *Location of Culture*, p. 86.
7 Bhabha, *Location of Culture*, p. 88.

being able to act their oppressor's part, if even only 'almost . . . but not quite'. Mimicry served an important function in the attainment of freedom, for it did serve to indicate capabilities of the colonized that the colonizer would have otherwise denied.

However, in the postcolonial era, with the attainment of political independence by the colonized nation-states and of autonomy and self-government by the churches, the colonial aims of mimicry having been achieved, the former colonized seem to have so learned the arts as to have continued performing them as if to convince themselves of their own success. Mimicry as a strategy for the subversion and overthrow of colonialism became a postcolonial way of life and, as Mbembe presents, sometimes exceeded the practice during the colonial period. In Africa, we are left especially in the churches with the repetition of the doctrines and negative attitudes of the colonizers towards all things African to the detriment and neglect of these rich traditions in the most serious attempts at postcolonializing. Mimicry as a postcolonializing strategy goes only so far.

Improvisation

In improvisation, persons utilize whatever they can find at hand to make the most of an inadequate situation. Improvisation is the creed of the slave, the colonized, the un-free who must make the most of what is available. The colonized, slaves and people kept under domination have used incredible skills to improvise. Improvisation in music, art and literature bears witness to the ingenuity and social fortitude of the oppressed. In terms of the colonial experience it seems to me that the colonized and especially the enslaved used improvisation to good effect as a survival strategy. As the need arose for the formulation of ceremonies at times especially of gathering, slaves no doubt used whatever was at hand and whatever they could call to memory in the crafting of rituals of encouragement, memorial and renewal. With limited resources of education in the languages of the colonizer, the colonized were still able, as for instance in the establishment of AICs,

Black churches and other Black spiritual movements, to form social institutions that resembled those of the colonizers whilst infusing them with the philosophies and cultural content of their African heritage.

Improvisation as a colonial and postcolonial activity differs from mimesis in that it includes substantial content from the cultural heritage of the colonized. As a postcolonializing exercise improvisation went much further than imitation. It entailed a degree of independence and unconcern with the gaze of the colonizer. In slavery, it happened mostly away from that gaze. In colonialism, it took place decidedly in contexts in which the influence of colonizers was very limited. Thus improvisation became a significant strategy of the free in which their dignity and capabilities were expressed and endorsed from within themselves and their own communities. Improvisation, I would suggest, continues to be a significant postcolonializing activity, but that of those whose resources, in both colonial and indigenous terms, are limited. Improvisation goes further than mimicry, but not far enough.

Creativity

In creativity the colonized have great facility in both their own arts and those of the colonizer. The creative person has inner freedom that is borne of confidence in different spheres and fields of knowledge. Such confidence comes from a variety of sources. The creative person is neither afraid of the sanctions of an authority nor has anxiety at the gaze of any legitimizing forerunner. Creativity is postcolonializing activity that has attained maturity. Developmentally I suggest that postcolonializing is often the end of a process that begins with imitation, matriculates through improvisation and then attains full flight in creativity.

My discussions of the Black Church and Black spirituality (Chapter 2), postcolonializing liturgy (Chapter 3), and the transcending of colonial religion (Chapter 4) demonstrate all three strategies of imitation, improvisation and creativity. In any postcolonializing activity, elements of all these three may be found.

A THEOLOGICAL IMPERATIVE

Practical theology in Africa has engaged all three forms. However, going forward in response to the postcolonializing God spoken about in Chapter 1, I suggest, calls for courageous postcolonializing activity, a significant example of which we discussed in Chapter 4. If African practical theology is to make the significant contribution it is well able to in enhancing global developments, then it will be in the forefront of the creation of liturgical rituals that draw significantly on the worldview and practices of Africa (Chapter 3). The nature of the care of persons it offers will draw on the spiritual and anthropological preferences of Africa (Chapter 5). Last but not least, it will cease from the nervous navel-gazing that has characterized other forms of practical theology and from the constant looking over its shoulder to see what former colonizers say and think of what it does. It will recognize how the God of all creation revels in diversity and seems to want to encourage it in every area of human life. With all the energy and faith it can muster, African practical theology must pursue and engage in the activities of postcolonializing God.

Bibliography

Anquandah, James K. (ed.), *The Trans Atlantic Slave Trade: Landmarks, Legacies, Expectations* (Proceedings of the International Conference on Historic Slave Routes held in Accra, Ghana, 30th August–2nd September, 2004), Accra, Ghana: Sub-Saharan Publishers, 2007.

Armah, Ayi Kwei, *The Healers: A Novel*, Popenguine, Senegal: Per Ankh, 2000.

Baëta, Christian G., *Prophetism in Ghana: A Study of Some 'Spiritual' Churches*, London: SCM Press, 1962.

Bediako, Kwame, *Christianity in Africa*, Edinburgh: Edinburgh University Press, 1995.

Bhabha, Homi K., *The Location of Culture*, London/New York: Routledge, 1994.

Boahen, A. Adu, *African Perspectives on Colonialism*, Baltimore, MD: Johns Hopkins University Press, 1987.

Césaire, Aimé, *Discourse on Colonialism*, translated by Joan Pinkham, New York: Monthly Review Press, 1972.

Chireau, Yvonne, 'Thirty Years after Slave Religion: The Circle of Culture', *SSBR [Society for the Study of Black Religion] Newsletter* (2006), pp. 3–5.

Chireau, Yvonne, *Black Magic: Religion and the African American Conjuring Tradition*, Berkeley: University of California Press, 2003.

Clarke, Clifton, 'Towards an African Post-Missionary Christology among African Indigenous Churches in Ghana', PhD Thesis, University of Birmingham, UK, 2003.

Davis, Kortright, *Emancipation still Comin': Explorations in Caribbean Emancipatory Theology*, New York: Orbis, 1982.

Du Bois, W. E. B., *The Souls of Black Folk*, Harmondsworth: Penguin, 1989 [1903].

Du Bois, W. E. B. (ed.), *The Negro Church*, a reprint of the 1903 edition with an Introduction by Phil Zuckerman, Sandra L. Barnes and Daniel Cady, New York: Alta Mira Press & Rowman & Littlefield, 2003 [1903].

Ephirim-Donkor, Anthony, *African Religion Defined: A Systematic Study of Ancestor Worship among the Akan*, New York/Toronto/Plymouth: University Press of America, 2013.
Fett, Sharla, *Working Cures: Healing, Health and Power on Southern Slave Plantations*, Chapel Hill & London: University of North Carolina Press, 2002.
Gyekye, Kwame, *African Cultural Values: An Introduction*, Lansing, MI: Sankofa, 1996.
Hurston, Zora Neale, *The Sanctified Church*, New York: Marlowe, 1981.
Keller, Catherine, Michael Nausner & Mayra Rivera (eds), *Postcolonial Theologies: Divinity and Empire*, St Louis, MO: Chalice Press, 2004.
Lartey, Emmanuel Y., *Pastoral Counselling in Inter-cultural Perspective*, Frankfurt/London/New York: Peter Lang, 1987.
Lartey, Emmanuel, *In Living Color: An Intercultural Approach to Pastoral Care and Counseling*, London: Jessica Kingsley, 1987.
Lartey, Emmanuel, 'Globalization, Internationalization and Indigenization of Pastoral Care and Counseling', in Nancy Ramsey (ed.), *Pastoral Care and Counseling: Redefining the Paradigms*, Nashville: Abingdon, 2004, pp. 87–108.
Levine, Lawrence, *Black Culture and Black Consciousness*, New York: Oxford University Press, 1977.
Mbembe, Achille, *On the Postcolony*, Berkeley/Los Angeles/London: University of California Press, 2001.
Memmi, Albert, *The Colonizer and the Colonized*, Boston: Beacon Press, 1965.
Moore-Gilbert, Bart, *Postcolonial Theory: Contexts, Practices, Politics*, London/New York: Verso, 1997.
Murphy, Joseph M., *Working the Spirit: Ceremonies of the African Diaspora*, Boston: Beacon Press, 2003 [1994].
Opoku, Kofi Asare, *West African Traditional Religion*, Singapore: FEP International, 1978.
Peel, John D. Y., *Aladura: A Religious Movement among the Yoruba*, Oxford University Press, 1968.
Pinn, Anthony, *Varieties of African American Religious Experience*, Minneapolis: Fortress Press, 1998.
Pobee, John S., *Toward an African Theology*, Nashville, TN: Abingdon, 1979.
Raboteau, Albert, *Slave Religion: The 'Invisible Institution' in the Antebellum South*, New York: Oxford University Press, 1978.
Ramsey, Nancy (ed.), *Pastoral Care and Counseling: Redefining the Paradigms*, Nashville, TN: Abingdon, 2004.
Said, Edward W., *The World, the Text, and the Critic*, London: Vintage, 1991.

Somé, Malidoma Patrice, *The Healing Wisdom of Africa: Finding Life Purpose through Nature, Ritual and Community*, New York: Jeremy P. Tarcher/Putnam, 1998.

Stewart, Dianne M., *Three Eyes for the Journey: African Dimensions of the Jamaican Religious Experience*, Oxford: Oxford University Press, 2005.

Stuckey, Sterling, *Slave Culture*, New York: Oxford University Press, 1987.

Sugirtharajah, R. S. (ed.), *The Postcolonial Biblical Reader*, Oxford/Malden/Carlton: Blackwell Publishing, 2006.

Sundkler, Bengt, *Bantu Prophets in South Africa*, Oxford: Oxford University Press, 1961 [1948].

Tetteh, Ishmael, *Soul Processing: The Path to Freedom. A Revolutionary Spiritual Mind Science for Total Well Being*, Accra: The Etherean Mission, 1997.

Tetteh, Ishmael, *The Fountain of Life: A Course in Metaphysics*, Accra, Ghana: The Etherean Mission, 1999.

Tetteh, Ishmael N. O., *The Inspired African Mystical Gospel*, Accra: Etherean Mission Publishing, 2001.

Tetteh, Ishmael N. O., *Etherean Mission Handbook*, Accra: Asante & Hittscher Press, n. d.

Tetteh, Ishmael, *The Mission of Jesus Revealed*, Accra: Etherean Mission Publishing, 2011.

Turner, Harold, *History of an African Independent Church*, London: Clarendon Press, 1967.

Westhelle, Vítor, *After Heresy: Colonial Practices and Post-colonial Theologies*, Eugene, OR: Cascade Books, 2010.

Index

adaptability 29–30
Africa
  independence vii
  mystical traditions 100–4
  newspapers xix–xx
  political parties xx
  spirituality viii, 30–1, 120
  theologians use colonialist method x–xi
  theology uses bodily expression 30
  traditional medicine 115–17
  traditional religions 25–31
African American Christianity 15–37
African Independent Churches viii
  and anticolonial campaigns xx–xxii
  as New Religious Movements 31–7
Akan society 42
ancestors 58, 60, 69, 102–3, 111, 112–13
  and libation 115
animal sacrifice 48
Armah, Ayi Kwei 116
astral influences 91–3
astral planes 98
authoritarian epistemology xii

Baalim 7–8
Baalot 7–8
Babel xviii, 1–4
Bhabha, Homi 125–6
Bible 71–2
  see also Babel; Good Samaritan; Syro-Phoenician woman

Black churches in the USA 15, 18
Black spirituality 18–25, 31–7
Boahen, Adu xviii–xxi
Brazil 22–3

Canaanite religion 7
Candomblé 22–3
Catherine, Mother 24–5
centurion, his faith 6–7
Césaire, Aimé xv
change xvii–xviii
chaplains, institutional 123
Chireau, Yvonne 23–4
Christ 75–6
Church of God in Christ 24
colonialism xviii–xxi
colonialist methods, and African theologians x–xi
communities of care 121
communotheism 27
Congo xix, xxi
Conjuring 23–4
cosmic harmony 28–9
counting 106
creativity 29–30, 128–9
  in Elmina Castle ceremony 62
  feature of African religions 33
creator 108
Cuba 22–3
culture, and identity 101, 103–4

Davis, Kortright 33
death, and re-birth 97–9

desire 83
devil 79–81
diasporan churches xi, xiii–xiv
disease, caused by soul 93
diversity xiii, xvii, 14
  of creation 2–3
  of human culture 3–4
Door of Return 46–7
drink offerings 113–15
drums 44
Du Bois, W. E. B. 15–16, 19

Elmina Castle 39
Ephirim-Donkor, Anthony 112
Etherean Mission xiv, 65–117
Ethiopian churches xx–xxi
Eurocentrism 34–5
evil 29

fasting 89
fertility rituals 8
Fett, Sharla 21
frenzy 5–16, 32–3

Garvey, Joseph 50
gender, God as Father-Mother 74, 111–12
Gerizim, Mount 9–10
Ghana xiv, xx, xxi–xxii
  Joseph Project 38–40
  Methodist churches xi
God
  African concepts of 72–4
  as creator 108
  embodied in nature 105, 107
  as Father-Mother 74, 111–12
  names of 106–7
gods, as messengers 108–12
Good Samaritan 9–11

Haiti 22–3
healing 16–17, 23–4, 43–4, 65, 91–3, 115–17

health 21, 91–3
hegemony
  countered in Ghana ceremony 57
  God acts to dispel 3–4
  questioned by postcolonialism xvi
  herbal remedies 92
heritage
  of African traditional religions 25–31, 68
  denial xi
hospitality 114
humanity 76–9
Hurston, Zora Neale 24, 32
hybridity 59–61

immigrant churches xi
improvisation 127–8
independence vii
indigeneity 118–19
indigenization 38
institutional chaplains 123
intelligence 77–9
internationalization 118

Jacob, offers a libation 114
Jamaica 22
James Fort 55
Jesus, and people of other faiths 4–11
Joseph Project 39–40

karma 83–5, 96
Katanga xxi
Kimbangu, Simon xxi
Kimbanguist churches xxi
Kitawala churches xxi

language see Babel
libation 49–50, 60, 102, 113–15
liberation 83–5
liturgy 38–64

Maji Maji rebellion xix
Marley, Rita 50

INDEX

Mason, C. H. 24
Mbembe, Achille xii
Mbiti, John S. 26
meditation 88
Memmi, Albert xv
mental colonization 103
Methodist churches xi
mimcry 125–6
mind 77–9, 81–2
Mokalapa, Willie J. xx
monotheism, and polytheism 105–6
moon god 111–12
mother earth 109–10
Mumbo cult xxi
Murphy, Joseph 19, 22–3
Musama Disco Christo Church xxi–xxii
music 47–8, 51
mysticism
  African traditions 100–4
  and communal ritual 28
  of Ishmael Tetteh 66–8

names of God 106–7
nation states vii
nature, as embodiment of God 105, 107
neo-colonialism vii
New Religious Movements, and African Independent Churches 31–7
newspapers xix–xx
Ngwale, Kinjiktile xix
Nigeria xx
Nkoie, Maria xix
numbering 106
Nyirenda, Tomo xxi

Obetsebi-Lamptey, Jake 39, 45, 48–9, 52, 53–6
Opoku, Kofi Asare 27
Osibisa (band) 47–8, 61

pain 95–6
pardon 52–3

pastoral care 118–23
Pentecost xviii, 14
Pentecostal churches xx, 23–4
Pinn, Anthony 19, 23
pluralism 14, 100
  religious 4–11
plurality
  in Ghana's Elmina Castle ceremony 60
  in spiritual and divine realm 27
Pobee, John 42–4, 49–50
political parties xx
politics, and pastoral care 122
polytheism, and monotheism 105–6
polyvocality xviii, 14, 61–2
possession 28
postcolonialism viii–x, xiii
  divine activities xxii, 1–14
prayer 86–8
  postures 114
preachers 16–17
priest-healers 16–17
prophet-healers 32
prosperity gospel 34

Raboteau, Albert 20–1
ram sacrifice 48
Rawlings, J. J. 42
re-birth 97–9
reconciliation 52, 53–4
reincarnation 83–5
relationality xvii
religious studies x
religious unity 99–100
remembrance 62–3
repentance 52
Revival Zion 22–3
ritual
  in African traditional religions 42–4
  and mysticism 28
Roman religion 6–7

sacredness of all life 26–7
sacrifice, ram 48

Said, Edward x
Samaritan religion 9–11
Santería 22–3
scriptures 71–2
Senegal xx
Shemites 1–2
sin 29, 42, 96
slave culture 17–18, 20
slavery
  revolts against 22
  silence over 57
Somé, Malidoma 43
soul
  cause of disease 93
  eternal 83–5
Soul Processing 85, 93–7
sound 89–91
spirit, of humankind 77
spiritual churches xx
Spiritualism 23–4
spirituality 120
Stewart, Dianne 22, 27

strategy
  in Ghana ritual 57–8
  of postcolonializing activities xvi–xvii
Stuckey, Sterling 17–18, 20
sun god 111–12
Syro-Phoenician woman 7–9

Tembu church xx
Tetteh, Ishmael 65–117, 125
therapy 120–1
Tile, Nehemiah xx
trance 28
Turner, Harold 35

United States 15–37

Vodou 22–3

Westhalle, Vitor 1
Winneba Youth Choir 51, 61

Zionist churches xxi

www.ingramcontent.com/pod-product-compliance
Lightning Source LLC
Chambersburg PA
CBHW070302010526
44108CB00039B/1645